I0569554

At *Mama*
Feely's Feet

Trauma, Truth, and the
Journey Back to Ourselves

This book is intended for educational and inspirational purposes only. It is not a substitute for professional mental health treatment. If you are experiencing emotional distress, trauma-related symptoms, or mental health challenges, please seek support from a licensed therapist or mental health provider in your area. If you are in crisis, call or text **988** to reach the **Suicide & Crisis Lifeline**, available 24/7.

Published in the United States by **Hope Venetta**.
Cover art and design by **Hope Venetta**.

Scripture quotations, unless otherwise noted, are from the **Holy Bible, English Standard Version (ESV)**, copyright © 2001 by Crossway, a publishing ministry of Good News Publishers. All rights reserved.

Dedication

To Mama Feely, and for every ancestor whose blood, breath, and prayers connect me to the Mafa people of present-day Cameroon, where my story begins. Your resilience endures in me. Your lives were not in vain.

Author's Note

My heart in writing this book was to humanize history. I wanted to take the facts, records, and fragments left to us and breathe life into them again—so that our people's voices would not be reduced to statistics or dates on a page.

In some places, the trail of my own family history ran cold. When that happened, I wove together what I did know with truths from the wider African American experience. In those moments, I chose to fictionalize portions of my personal history, but always with care: drawing from the documented lives, struggles, and resilience of our ancestors.

This book is not meant to blur the line between fact and fiction, but to fill in the silences left by time. Every story told here is grounded in truth—whether from the record of my own lineage or from the collective story of our people.

Table of Contents

Introduction

I didn't realize how wounded I was. For years I moved through life oblivious to the pain buried inside me. As Black women, we're taught to do that, aren't we? We press forward as if nothing's wrong, even when our souls are aching. It's like getting a cut that scabs over before the skin underneath truly heals. That was me. My heart was covered by scabs that allowed me to function, or so I believed, while the deeper wound festered unseen.

It wasn't until the upheaval of 2020 that the truth broke open. Pressure had been building around those wounds for years, and then all at once the anguish surged out like a torrent.

For so long, I lacked the words to explain what I was feeling. My emotions, long suppressed, rose up with a force that demanded attention. Writing this book became part of how I answered that call. The process has been both painful and tender. I have cried. Sometimes with sorrow, sometimes with relief. What I've learned is not to stew in my emotions or try to silence them, but to acknowledge them fully and then release them. That rhythm of naming and letting go has become vital to my healing.

None of these wounds are new. They've built upon one another over time, layer after layer, like sediment pressing down through the generations. Which raises the deeper question: where did it all start? How did our pain, both personal and collective, take root?

In my field, we often talk about *Adverse Childhood Experiences*, or ACEs. These are the kinds of early injuries that leave a lasting imprint on body and mind. Emotional neglect. Witnessing violence. Growing up around addiction or mental illness. For many of us, this isn't clinical jargon—it's lived experience.

When those experiences stack up without safety or support, they shape us in ways we don't always recognize. They can alter how we see ourselves, how easily we trust others, and even how our bodies hold stress. But ACEs aren't meant to box us in or define us. Their purpose is to give us language. To help us name what hurt us, so we can finally begin to heal.

Because when we don't tend to these wounds, they don't simply vanish. They echo forward. They ripple into our relationships, our communities, and even our biology.

But what happens when it's not just one person's story?
What happens when generation after generation grows up in homes marked by trauma. Where silence, instability, or violence become part of the family rhythm? Not because anyone chooses it, but because it's all that's been known?

This is where we begin to talk about *intergenerational trauma.*

As trauma therapist Resmaa Menakem explains:

"Many times trauma in a person decontextualized over time can look like personality. Trauma in a family decontextualized over time can look like family traits. Trauma decontextualized in a people over time can look like culture…"

Our inherited wounds show up in ways both subtle and obvious. They're in the warnings wrapped in love, like "the talk" we give our sons about police encounters. They're in the stress our grandmothers swallowed so they could endure another day. They're in the way our bodies still clench and brace, even when the threat has long passed.

Intergenerational trauma happens when the wounds of one generation ripple into the next, not only through behaviors, but also through biology. Science is beginning to confirm what our bodies have always known. *Epigenetics*, the study of how stress and trauma affect gene expression, shows that trauma can literally imprint itself on our DNA. It can influence how our nervous systems respond, how our immune systems function, and how emotions are carried forward across time.

For those of us descended from enslaved Africans in the United States, this truth is undeniable. Much of what we've normalized as "just who we are", the hypervigilance, the constant over-functioning, the way we swallow our truth, are not simply quirks of personality. They are survival strategies. They were once necessary to keep our people alive.

Now, the invitation is to slow down and ask: what still serves us, and what is quietly stealing our peace?

As a psychotherapist on this healing and writing journey, I find myself returning again and again to the same questions: How have the events of the past continued to echo into the present? How are they shaping not only our lives today but the future of our children? The answers are never simple. Trauma is rarely simple. Still, this book is my attempt to trace the threads, to name the origins of our suffering, and to point toward a path of healing.

Our story, as descendants of enslaved Africans in this land, begins in 1619. The first Africans arrived on the shores of Jamestown and were stripped of names, languages, families, and faith practices. Every thread of identity was torn loose, deliberately and systematically. The process of dehumanization didn't happen in a single act. It unfolded slowly, over generations.

At first, Africans were seen as laborers—enslaved, but still recognized as human. But as time went on, laws were written, customs hardened, and myths crafted to justify exploitation. What happened wasn't accidental. Psychological studies remind us how easily ordinary people can be conditioned to harm others when given permission, power, or pressure. The Milgram experiments. The Stanford Prison Study. We've seen how cruelty can be normalized when systems reward obedience over empathy.

And what was the system at play? Unbridled capitalism, but we'll get to that later. Gradually, our ancestors were recast as property. Beasts of burden. Units of profit. This wasn't just a physical stripping away; it was emotional, spiritual, and psychological warfare. Designed not only to control the body. Oh no, this was to crush the soul because the oppressor trained himself to believe we had no soul.

And yet, even under that weight, our ancestors endured.

Let's be clear about something: the trauma didn't end when slavery did. Wounds that deep didn't simply close with emancipation. They carried forward, woven into the fabric of daily life, and compounded by what came next. Jim Crow laws. Segregation. Economic disenfranchisement. Each era layered new injuries on top of old ones.

The civil rights movement of the 1960s was a beacon of hope, yet even its victories could not erase centuries of pain. Freedom marches and legislation changed laws, but they could not fully mend the generational wounds left by slavery's shadow.

And the pain has never been confined to the past. It is still unfolding around us. We see it in the murders of Breonna Taylor, Ahmaud Arbery, George Floyd, and so many others. We see it in the rise of nationalism, fascism, and white supremacy across the United States. For many of us, these tragedies were not isolated events but fresh wounds layered atop ancestral ones. They pulled long-buried grief to the surface—grief that demanded to be witnessed, not only by the world, but by ourselves.

In the aftermath of these collective traumas, something sacred has been rising among us. As of the writing of this book, Black women across the country are declaring 2025 the year of rest. Not retreat, but restoration. No more apologizing for sitting down. No more carrying guilt for not being the first to respond, organize, fix, or fight.

This moment has been building for years. Cultural voices like The Nap Ministry, founded by Tricia Hersey, have reminded us that rest is not weakness—it is resistance. Rest disrupts white supremacy. Rest reclaims our divine worth. Hersey's words have taken on new urgency in our time, as exhaustion threatens to become our default.

And so, on March 10, 2025—Harriet Tubman Day—Black women across the nation observed the first *National Day of Rest for Black Women*. It was a sacred pause. A way of honoring a woman who carried so many others to freedom, while remembering that our liberation also depends on learning to carry ourselves with tenderness and care.

This isn't laziness. This is strategy. This is survival. This is healing. We are re-learning what it means to be fully human, to breathe deeply, to feel safe in our own bodies. We are done waiting for permission.

As Black American women, our stories are layered with the weight of both race and gender. We have carried unique burdens—our labor exploited, our bodies fetishized and devalued. We have been the backbone of our families and communities, yet too often overlooked and underappreciated. Our strength has been our armor, but also our burden, as we navigate a society that seeks to diminish our worth at every turn.

The rise in racial violence has forced these realities back into sharp focus. The murders of Black men and women at the hands of police, captured on camera and broadcast around the world, were not random tragedies. They were the latest in a long line of violations against our people. Their deaths tore open wounds that had never healed.

And yet, even in grief, our communities rose. The protests and uprisings that followed were not simply about one life or one death. They were a collective cry for justice. A demand to be seen and heard. A reckoning with the systems that have tried for centuries to silence us.

In writing this book, I've had to confront not only my own pain but the pain of my ancestors. The process has been deeply emotional—filled with moments of sorrow, anger, but ultimately, hope.

I have cried for the women who came before me. For the mothers and daughters who endured unthinkable suffering yet found the strength to press forward. I have cried for myself and for the women of my generation who are still fighting to claim our rightful place in a world that often seeks to erase us. I have even cried for the women of tomorrow, wondering if they, too, will inherit these same burdens.

And yet, each tear has reminded me that we are still here. That survival itself is testimony. That in our pain there is also resilience, and in our grief there is also love.

But this book is not just about pain. It is also about healing, empowerment, and resilience. It is about reclaiming our heritage and finding strength in our faith. It is about remembering that trauma does not define us. It is part of our story, but it is not the whole story. When we face our wounds honestly, we create the possibility of healing. And when we heal, we make space for a different future, for ourselves and for the generations that follow.

Still, I wrestled with how to speak about trauma without burying us under clinical labels. People connect with stories, not diagnoses. So let's try an experiment. Let me show you what trauma can look like in real life. These aren't textbook symptoms; these are lived realities. The names may not be yours, but the struggles might feel familiar.

Tiana gripped the steering wheel so tightly her knuckles ached, the engine humming in Park. Another argument with her sister—this time about whose turn it was to check on Mama—had erupted into full-blown rage. The fury had come like fire, hot and sharp. She had screamed, slammed a door, then collapsed into shame. *Why do I always do this?* Her thoughts spiraled. *Why can't I just stay calm?* Her forehead rested on the wheel, body trembling, bone-weary from an emotional rollercoaster she could not escape.

Carla leaned into the cool granite countertop, her arms trembling from the effort to stay upright. Another wave of nausea gripped her, sharp and sudden. She clutched her stomach and breathed through her teeth. The doctors had run every test—blood, imaging, specialists. Always the same conclusion: "There's nothing physically wrong."

But Carla knew better. Her body had always spoken the truths she was too scared to name. As a child, she had flinched at slammed doors, braced herself at the sound of footsteps. That constant fear had lived in her muscles for decades.

Now, in her 30s, the fear showed up as migraines, jaw pain, chest tightness that mimicked a heart attack. She had come to dread the mornings—when she awoke to pain before she'd even moved. Some days, just brushing her teeth felt like pushing a boulder uphill. Her body was a battlefield, still fighting a war long since ended.

Serena sat cross-legged on the edge of her bed, lit only by the blue glow of her phone. The screen buzzed again, another unread message. She stared at it, then turned the phone face down. Her heart raced with guilt, but her fingers felt frozen. *They don't really care,* she told herself. *They'll leave eventually, like everyone else.*

Her last relationship had unraveled slowly, poisoned by her own doubt. She replayed every fight, every "Where are you?" text she'd sent, each time she questioned a harmless glance or a late reply. She knew it was too much. But she couldn't stop.

Raised in a house where love had to be earned and stability was a myth, Serena had learned early not to trust joy. Silence felt safer than vulnerability. Distance felt safer than hope. And now, that illusion of safety was suffocating her.

Deja's fingers hovered over her keyboard, unmoving. The words on the screen blurred. A sharp smell—coffee and printer ink—morphed into that of asphalt and sweat. In an instant, she wasn't in her office anymore.

She was twelve again, hiding behind a fence, watching as officers tackled her childhood friend. She saw the boot, the crack of the gun, the way his body went still.

She blinked, but the past clung to her skin like heat. Her breath came in short gasps. The clock on the wall ticked, but she couldn't feel time passing. These moments came without warning.

Afterward, she would sit motionless, unsure where she was or who she had become. The trauma wasn't just in her memories—it had taken root in her nervous system. She felt fractured, living a half-life somewhere between yesterday and today.

Jasmine's keys jingled in her trembling hand as she yanked open the door. The walls of her apartment felt like they were closing in. The argument with her boyfriend still echoed in her head; accusations, slammed doors, too many "always" and "never"s. Her heart pounded like it was trying to escape.

She didn't think, just drove. Ended up at the same bar as always, neon lights flickering like sirens. The first drink burned going down. The second numbed her edges. By the third, she was laughing too loudly, leaning too close to a stranger who smelled like cologne and something dangerous.

Every flirtation, every shot was a small rebellion against the emptiness she carried. But by midnight, the buzz turned bitter. Her reflection in the bathroom mirror looked like a stranger.

Why do I do this to myself? she whispered. But the silence had no answer.

All of the above sound like women we all know and love, right? They might even sound like us. Friends, the stories of Tiana, Carla, Serena, Deja, and Jasmine are descriptions of what Complex Post-Traumatic Stress Disorder (CPTSD) can look like.

CPTSD develops when a person is exposed to ongoing trauma over long periods of time, often beginning in childhood. Unlike PTSD, which can result from a single traumatic event, CPTSD grows out of repeated wounding—abuse, neglect, violence in the home, instability, or environments where safety is never guaranteed. Its effects show up in many ways: intense emotions that feel uncontrollable, difficulty trusting others, physical pain without a clear medical cause, and a body that never seems to rest.

African Americans may experience CPTSD at higher rates than other groups because our trauma is both historical and ongoing. The constant strain of systemic racism, discrimination, and oppression creates a pattern of stress that is passed down across generations. It isn't always one traumatic event that breaks us. It is the repetition. Being watched while shopping. Being followed through certain neighborhoods. Being denied opportunities or dismissed when asking for help. These aren't isolated slights; they are patterns of dehumanization.

Our trauma is layered. It is personal and inherited, shaped by forced migration, stolen land, stolen labor, and stolen lives. It is reinforced in modern times by police brutality, medical neglect, wage gaps, food deserts, and school systems that criminalize instead of nurture. None of these realities stand alone. Together they create a web of chronic injustice that wears down the body, the mind, and the spirit, making us more vulnerable to the weight of CPTSD.

When hypervigilance becomes a family trait, when the nervous system never gets to rest, when survival skills are passed from mother to daughter—that is not just stress. That is trauma.

There's no way around it, this book is about CPTSD. But I want you to know from the beginning: my approach is not about pinning you to a diagnostic label. Too often, what gets stamped as a *disorder* is actually a logical response to prolonged pressure, pain, or oppression.

Think about it. What if hypervigilance isn't "anxiety" but a skill learned from growing up in a world where safety was never promised? What if emotional numbness isn't dysfunction but a shield, carefully built after too many heartbreaks? These responses may look pathological on paper, but in context they are wisdom— strategies of survival.

The problem is that instead of exploring the story behind our pain, too often we're handed pills without understanding, or diagnoses without compassion. We are told what's wrong with us but rarely in context to what *happened* to us. That's what this book seeks to change.

Because no matter what we carry—rage, grief, shame, exhaustion—we all want the same thing: to be seen as fully human. We don't need a clinical manual that feels detached from our lives. We need a witness. We need truth-telling that honors our context.

This book is also about decolonizing knowledge. You see, the way we've been taught to revere the written record of history as the ultimate proof of truth is not neutral. That, too, is a product of white supremacy. Our African ancestors did not reduce wisdom to ink on a page. Knowledge lived in bodies, in voices, in drums, in dance. It was spoken, sung, remembered, performed.

The role of the griot

Griots didn't just tell history, they *embodied* it. Their voices carried the spirit of a people across generations. Memory was not archived in silence; it was activated in community. But under colonial power, the written word was elevated above all else: fixed, owned, controlled. Oral traditions were cast as unreliable, uncivilized, even dangerous. And slowly, many of us internalized that lie. We learned to trust citation over testimony, print over story, distance over presence.

So yes, even in writing this book, I wrestle with contradiction. I am using a tool that was not built for me. Sometimes the language feels foreign—too tight, too cold, too far from the rhythm of how we truly speak and know.

But I write anyway.

Because reclaiming voice, even on the page, is its own act of resistance.
Because our truths deserve to be heard as well as read.
Because if the written word has been used to distort us, it can also be used to restore us when we bring our whole selves to it.

So no, I don't claim this is the only way to tell our story. But it is *one* way. And even here, I honor the ancestors whose mouths never stopped moving, even when their words were never written down. Their wisdom still hums in our bones. Their folkways, languages, and mores were pressed into silence, yet they remain in our cells, in our memories, waiting to be remembered.

That's what this healing journey is about: reclaiming what is already within us. We've been conditioned to keep looking outward for validation, for proof that we matter. But the time has come to look inward. To trust that our knowing is enough.

And it is here that I introduce Mama Feely.

Mama Feely is more than a character. She is a composite shaped by one of my own ancestors and the stories of countless enslaved women. She is a griot, a guide, a spiritual anchor for those of us descended from enslaved Africans in the United States. Through her, I hope to explore self-discovery, emotional healing, empowerment, and the reconnection to identities that were stripped away. Her voice will walk with us through these pages, giving shape to truths that history tried to bury.

Here's my challenge - how to portray Mama Feely's voice. Should I use the the vernacular used among enslaved Black people in the 19th century, offering a historically accurate and immersive experience? Or adopt a more flowery delivery typical of that time period, adding a poetic touch? Perhaps use today's vernacular, ensuring her wisdom and insights are easily digestible for modern readers?

I look at other writers like Zora Neale Hurston and Toni Morrison, who masterfully use "broken" English and African American vernacular. By no means am I comparing myself to these incredible icons, but I understand that such language can be challenging to read with today's understanding of English. Should I even attempt it? I'm still not sure. In the end, my goal is to avoid turning Mama Feely into a caricature while making sure her voice resonates and is comprehensible to my readers. This creative struggle is not just about language; it's about honoring the legacy of those who came before us and ensuring their stories are told with the respect and clarity they deserve. I hope I've done her justice.

And before we go any further, I need to tell you plainly: yes, there will be some Jesus in these pages. This book is rooted in Christian faith. But not the kind of faith that has been twisted to shame us, silence us, or keep us in bondage. I'm talking about the faith that liberates. The faith that makes room for your questions, your grief, even your anger—and still points you toward hope.

I write as someone who knows what it means to pray through pain, to wrestle with Scripture when it doesn't seem to soothe, to sit in the tension between believing and doubting. Whether your faith feels steady, fragile, or scarred by harm you've experienced in church spaces, you are welcome here.

We will talk about trauma and history, but we will also talk about grace, redemption, and the God who never stopped seeing us.

This book was born out of the soil of our shared struggle and watered with the tears of generations. It is both testimony and offering—a guide for finding peace in the midst of chaos, rootedness in the face of disconnection, and truth in a world that has tried again and again to rewrite us.

And I need you to know: you do not walk this path alone. As we journey together, I hold close the words of the Apostle Paul in 2 Corinthians 4:8–9:

We are hard pressed on every side, but not crushed; perplexed, but not in despair; persecuted, but not abandoned; struck down, but not destroyed.

Yes, our wounds run deep. But our spirits? Deeper still. And within us lies the power to disrupt the cycle, to rise with intention, and to plant seeds of hope for those who come next.

This is more than a book. It is a reclamation. A remembering. A return.

Welcome to *At Mama Feely's Feet: Trauma, Truth and the Journey Back to Ourselves.*

May these pages feel like balm.

May they stir something sacred in you.

And may they remind you: healing is not only possible—it is your birthright.

Part 1: The Reckoning

CHAPTER 1

Navigating Trauma in a Rapid-Fire World

Before We Begin

Sis, I want to pause right here at the start and say, I see you. I see the way you've kept going, even when it's been hard. Even when your spirit was tired, even when the world around you felt like it was falling apart, you showed up. Maybe after reading the previous chapter, you realize you didn't know it was trauma you were carrying. Maybe you thought you were the problem. That you were just tired, frustrated, or on edge all the time because there was something wrong with you.

But I want you to know something: You're not broken. You are responding to a world that hasn't always been kind or safe, and you're still here.

This chapter is an invitation to exhale. To begin naming what you've carried and how it's shown up in your life. We're going to talk about some hard things, but I promise to walk with you through it gently, honestly, and anchored in faith. Like Jesus said in John 16:33: "In this world, you will have trouble. But take heart, I have overcome the world." And if He's overcome it, then there is hope for our healing too. Even here. Even now.

When the World Caught Fire

It started like any other morning. The soft clink of the spoon in my teacup. The quiet hum of the world waking up. I used to think starting the day with the news made me responsible, like being informed was a form of good citizenship. But in 2020, the headlines weren't just news anymore. They felt like spiritual attacks.

The death count from COVID was climbing. The world economy was reeling. But for me, like for so many Black women, the breaking point came with the murder of Ahmaud Arbery. Then Breonna Taylor. Then George Floyd. One name after another. In rapid succession. Each scroll through my social feeds felt like the breath had been knocked out of me. It was too much. And yet, I couldn't look away.

I remember sitting at my kitchen table in the quiet of the morning, tea in hand, already feeling that tightness in my chest. A dread crept in from the moment I'd open my phone or turn on the television. The stories of violence, political chaos, and relentless loss were like a faucet that wouldn't turn off. The TV might've been silent, but the trauma still leaked in through group chats, tweets, headlines, and side comments at work.

It was like the very air had become toxic. These insidious events of the 2010s and 2020s snaked their way into everything—like a predator threatening to choke the life out of anyone it could.

And yet, despite it all, I was still expected to show up to work and perform at my best.
Meet deadlines. Smile on video calls. Be productive. Be composed. Be *fine*.

But how could I be?
How does one compartmentalize grief that keeps renewing itself?
How do you concentrate when your spirit is splintering?

The world was on fire, and somehow, I was supposed to respond to emails like nothing was burning.

So I wrote about it.

I remember a Facebook post I shared during that summer of anguish: *"In this environment that moves lightning fast with developments on all fronts: COVID-19, politics, social unrest, career trajectory, I feel like I can't stop. Can't stop to process. Can't stop to feel. Can't stop to grow. Can't stop to connect with myself or connect with God."*

That post was a confession—and a cry.

The truth was, I wasn't just overwhelmed. I was angry. Furious. And beneath that anger lived something deeper: fear.

I was afraid of losing loved ones to a virus that didn't care how careful we were.

I was afraid of what the country was becoming, and what it had always been.

I was afraid for my Blackness. My body. My breath.

I didn't have the language then, but now I know: I was in survival mode. And that numbness? That irritability? That feeling like I was emotionally drowning? That's what unprocessed trauma does. It builds up in the body, layer after layer, until it starts leaking out; in our sleep, our relationships, our spirit.

Even as a therapist, someone trained to spot trauma patterns, I missed the signs in myself. The tight knot in my stomach. The racing thoughts. The sense of dread when I heard sirens or scrolled social media. That wasn't just stress. That was trauma doing what trauma does: keeping me on high alert, as if the danger never ended.

I knew I had to make a change. So, I stopped watching the news. I chose to protect my peace instead. I started my mornings with prayer, reflection, and time in the garden. I turned toward my family, my faith, the steady rhythms of life that reminded me I was still here. I carved out stillness, not because the world stopped hurting, but because I needed to stop bleeding.

But even then, it felt inescapable. No matter how far I tried to step back, the news still found me.

It echoed in my social feeds, in conversations with friends, in the weight I carried at church and at work. The murder of George Floyd wasn't just a story, it was a megaphone, a magnifying glass. It was a crack that split the dam wide open. The grief was collective. The rage was generational.

And I wasn't the only one feeling it.

In post after post, conversation after conversation, I heard Black women like me echoing the same exhaustion:

"I'm tired, but I can't stop."

"I'm scared, but I have to keep smiling."

"I'm grieving, but I still have a job to do."

That summer, I realized I couldn't think, pray, or hustle my way out of trauma. I needed support. I needed community. I needed to heal. So I began the hard work:

therapy. A support group. Boundaries. Rest. And more than anything—I began reclaiming the right to feel, to break down, and to rebuild.

I also created something I didn't even know I needed: a sister circle. In the middle of the mess, I invited a handful of Black women I trusted to come sit with me— right in my backyard. Over the years my husband and I had slowly turned our yard into an oasis: flowering plants in pretty pots, soft outdoor curtains draped from a wooden pergola, a gentle fountain burbling nearby, hummingbirds dipping in and out. Atmosphere matters when you're trying to breathe again. We made sure there was enough comfortable seating so no one had to perch or pretend. We wanted rest to be real.

We met outside, under the open sky, and gave ourselves permission to be seen. We read Dr. Rheeda Walker's *The Unapologetic Guide to Black Mental Health* and let her words spark brave conversations. The title says it all. Her insights truly set me free. Approaching mental health from an African American perspective was what I needed to understand myself and to let go of the lies the dominant culture had told me—that my pain was a personal failing. It wasn't. It isn't. It's a systemic failing. And seeing it clearly was the beginning of liberation.

I hope this book you're reading now can build on Dr. Walker's work and stand proudly beside the growing library of mental health resources created with Black people in mind and heart. Her book was like a mirror we didn't know we needed. We talked, we laughed, we cried. We held space for each other's stories—no judgment, no fixing, just presence. That sister circle became sacred ground, and her words helped till the soil.

And let me be clear: I didn't wait until I had everything perfectly figured out. I didn't wait until I was fully healed or professionally sanctioned to gather a circle. I just knew we needed it. And you don't need to wait either. Maybe this book can be the spark for your own sister circle. Maybe it already is.

You don't have to wait for permission. I didn't. And I'm so glad.

That's what brought me back to myself.

But I also want to be honest with you about how this trauma showed up in my body. Between 2020 and 2025, I experienced the worst flare-ups of my autoimmune disorder that I've ever had. The inflammation was out of control. Some days, I could barely get out of bed. I was crippled by pain and even hospitalized once. And while there are medical reasons for my condition, I know in my bones that holding onto years of unacknowledged anger and fear played a role.

There is growing scientific evidence that connects chronic stress, suppressed anger, and inflammation. I'm about to get a little nerdy, but bear with me. According to researchers from Harvard Health and the University of Rochester Medical Center, prolonged emotional suppression can overactivate the body's stress response systems, particularly the hypothalamic-pituitary-adrenal (HPA) axis, leading to increased inflammatory markers and worsening symptoms in autoimmune conditions like rheumatoid arthritis or lupus. Now, that doesn't mean scientists are saying stress automatically causes disease; what they've found is that the two often show up together, and that connection is too important to ignore.

When we constantly silence our pain or bottle up our emotions to survive racism, sexism, and everyday microaggressions, our bodies absorb that tension. We carry it in our joints, in our immune systems, in our hearts. I didn't always know how to name what I was feeling, especially when it came to anger, but I've learned that acknowledging it is the first step to letting it move through. Anger isn't wrong or inherently sinful. It's sacred information. It tells us that something matters.

And for years, I didn't let it speak.

Now, I'm learning to listen.

That's what rooted me again in who I am—not just as a professional, but as a descendant of enslaved Africans. A woman with a legacy of survival and a calling to turn survival into restoration.

The truth is, so many of us are walking around with spiritual whiplash and emotional exhaustion, mistaking it for personal weakness. But it's not weakness. It's *wounding*. The weight we carry is real and it didn't start with us. That wounding isn't just personal, it's patterned. And to understand the depth of what we carry, we have to look at the echoes of trauma passed down through generations, shaping how we show up in our bodies and in the world.

The Weight We Carry Together: Collective Trauma

What we lived through starting in 2020 wasn't just hard, it has been historic. And not the kind of history that gets tucked into a textbook and forgotten. It's been the kind that marks your nervous system. The kind that reshapes how you breathe, how you pray, how you feel in your own skin.

That's because the trauma wasn't just personal. It was *collective.*

Collective trauma happens when an entire community, people, or nation is wounded all at once. It disrupts the social fabric and shakes what we thought was stable—our faith in institutions, our sense of safety, our connection to each other.

It happens during pandemics. It happens during war. It happens in the aftermath of police killings, when you see a video you didn't ask to watch but can't look away from. It happens when you realize that your pain is not isolated, it's woven into the grief of your people.

And for Black folks in America, collective trauma didn't start in 2020.
It started on slave ships.
It was reinforced on the auction blocks, with the whips, in the laws.
It was encoded in the endurance of our grandmothers.
It was passed down in the stress hormones that still flood our bodies generations later.

What Science Confirms, We Already Knew

As we explored earlier, trauma changes the body. And those changes can be inherited. Through the field of epigenetics, researchers like Dr. Rachel Yehuda have shown that children and grandchildren of trauma survivors often carry stress responses shaped by events they never personally experienced.

That's why a protest on the news can feel like a panic attack.

That's why the sound of sirens can bring tears.

That's why you might feel emotionally raw—even when nothing "just happened."

Your body knows.

It remembers the collective pain we've carried as a people.

What Collective Trauma Looks Like

Emotional Exhaustion

I know I have been mentioning George Floyd a lot, but his death was pivotal. When he was murdered, something cracked open in the soul of this nation and in many of us. The grief was deep and familiar. It was layered with centuries of mourning.

You may have found yourself unable to focus.

Feeling like joy was out of reach.

Spending hours scrolling, crying, or numbing out.

Disrupted Relationships

You may have felt distance growing between you and people you once loved, people you considered allys, friends, coworkers, even church members because of silence, defensiveness, or dismissiveness about racism.

Maybe you tried to explain, to share your pain, only to be met with blank stares or platitudes. That hurt is real. That sense of betrayal is valid.

For many Black Americans, political and social tensions have led to difficult reckonings within our families and communities. Conversations about police violence, systemic injustice, and Black lives have caused ruptures, not only with white peers but sometimes within Black households as well. Writer Rainesford Stauffer notes that shifts in political identity can leave people feeling alienated or abandoned by family members they once trusted. Similarly, an NPR story titled "Dude, I'm Done" explores how racial justice movements have split households and tested long-standing friendships across the country.

Within the Black community, these rifts can feel even more complicated. Some of us were raised in politically conservative or religiously traditional homes where speaking out felt dangerous. Others were shocked to discover that friends or elders they admired dismissed our pain as 'overreacting.' These breaks in relational trust hurt—and healing them takes time, clarity, and sometimes distance.

Hypervigilance and Burnout

You might have found yourself holding your breath every time you stepped outside, even if you couldn't explain why. Maybe you noticed the tension creeping into everyday spaces: at the grocery store, in staff meetings on Zoom, even during Sunday worship. You weren't imagining it. You were bracing. Preparing yourself for the next offhand comment, the next injustice trending online, the next story of someone who looked like you being harmed, dismissed, or ignored.

That constant sense of alertness isn't paranoia, it's the nervous system doing exactly what it was trained to do. When you've lived through enough moments of not being safe; whether personally or through the collective grief of your community, your body learns to stay ready. Even when you're not in immediate danger, your mind and body might still be scanning the room, reading tone, calculating risk.

This isn't because you're broken. It's because you've adapted. You've learned, often without even realizing it, how to anticipate harm before it arrives. That kind of vigilance isn't easy to unlearn, especially when the threats, subtle or overt, still exist. But naming it is the first step. Because when you can name what's happening in your body, you can begin to tend to it with compassion instead of shame.

Spiritual Crisis

For some of us, 2020 and beyond has shaken our relationship with God to the core. The suffering was so loud, so visible, so relentless it stirred questions many of us had been carrying quietly for years. Where are You, Lord? Why do You let this happen? How long must we wait for justice?

These are not new questions. They echo the cries of the prophets and psalmists throughout scripture. *"How long, O Lord? Will You forget me forever?"* (Psalm 13:1). *"Even when I call out or cry for help, He shuts out my prayer."* (Lamentations 3:8). These aren't signs of lost faith—they are the language of lament. And lament is a sacred part of faith.

In the Black church tradition, we've often found ways to keep singing through sorrow, to shout in the valley. But even the most steadfast believer can feel spiritually disoriented in the face of such trauma. It's not wrong to question. Questioning is faith that hasn't given up.

When I couldn't feel God near me, I leaned on the knowledge that so many who came before me had cried out too and still pressed on. That became my hope: not in perfection, but in presence. A God who listens. A God who weeps. A God who remembers. That's the God who carried me through.

And if you're still asking those questions, you're not alone. You're in good, biblical company. Keep asking. Keep reaching. He can hold it.

You're Not Broken

If you saw yourself in any of this, I want you to hear me clearly:
You're not broken.
You're not too sensitive.
You're not "doing too much."

You are a mirror reflecting a deep, communal wound. And that means the healing won't be solitary either.

This is why community matters. Why story matters. Why reclaiming our heritage and our faith together matters. Because collective trauma can only be healed through collective restoration; through witness, through truth-telling, through walking each other back home to ourselves.

Reflection

When have you felt the weight of our collective grief most heavily?

Was it a moment in the news? A silence in your church? A conversation that fell flat?

How did your body respond? What did your spirit need?

This chapter has been about what happens when we finally stop running from our pain, and instead, turn toward it with open eyes and trembling hands. In a world that keeps breaking our hearts, I chose to stop numbing, stop pretending, and start healing.

And what carried me through that unraveling, what steadied me when nothing else could, was this promise from Jesus: "In this world, you will have trouble. But take heart; I have overcome the world" (John 16:33). The Greek word translated as "trouble" in that passage—*thlipsis*—means affliction, pressure, distress. It sounds an awful lot like what we now call trauma. Jesus didn't sugarcoat it. He didn't say we *might* have trouble. He said we *will*. He acknowledged the cold, hard truth of this broken world.

But then, He told us to take heart.

Not because the world isn't hard, but because He has already overcome it.

That truth gave me so much hope. Not naïve optimism, but real, soul-deep hope. The Lord of the universe, the One who sees everything we've been through, has already conquered the darkness. He doesn't promise us a pain-free life, but He does promise His presence, His victory, and His peace.

And that, dear reader, was enough to hold me steady while everything else was shaking. I acknowledged my rage, my grief, my fear, and I reached out for help. Therapy, rest, boundaries, and community became my oxygen. That was my beginning.

In the next chapter, I'll take you deeper into how my identity began to root and reshape how I stopped seeing myself as an orphan of history, and began reclaiming my place in a powerful, enduring lineage. Because healing doesn't just look forward, it looks back, too.

CHAPTER 2

From Orphan to Griot

Understanding and addressing trauma is the first step toward healing, but healing is a multifaceted journey that extends beyond individual introspection. As we embark on the next phase of this journey, we will delve into the transformative power of our roots. Just as acknowledging our pain and seeking support provides a foundation for resilience, so too can the stories of our ancestors. Rooting us, giving us a sense of place and purpose. By embracing our family histories, we can bridge the gap between past and present, turning feelings of loss and disconnection into a sense of belonging and purpose. So, let's get started with a crazy thing I found out about my husband.

Several years ago, I found that my husband can trace his lineage back 3 and a half centuries. Yes, centuries! His family historians have traced their lineage back to 1650 to a town in Italy. I was amazed when I heard this and saw the documentation. I was also sad and a bit jealous when thinking about myself in comparison. At the time, I barely knew who my grandparents were. He has a rich heritage he can grasp and see all around him. While he was growing up, the immigrant community from the town in the Old Country would have a yearly gathering called St Rocco's picnic after the patron saint of Collelongo, the town where his people are from. From looking at pictures and home movies of the event, it looked much like a family reunion. Whether they recognized it or not, this event, the connection to their place of origin served as a grounding force in their lives. In comparison, I felt like an orphan. No, frankly, I felt robbed. To be honest, I WAS robbed. My ancestors were stolen, sold, and shipped thousands of miles from anything familiar. Stripped of their languages and food. Ripped from their customs, and culture. This immense disconnection from my roots sparked a longing to understand my ancestors' stories.

Wanting what my husband had (and probably took for granted), I began my journey of growth and learning. I dove into discovering my blackness and my history. In investigating the history of the US, my own personal family history, coupled with my training in mental health, study of theology, and my own personal faith in Christ, I was able to find an anchor to who I am. No longer an orphan, but a daughter who comes from a people, and is loved by her Creator.

For many African Americans, there are no clear records. No names. No faces. We are unmoored. Relying on the here and now and our own creativity to fill in for a rootedness to something ancient. In 2016 that changed for me. I found a connection.

In 2016, several people on my mother's side got together and began research of our family history. They revealed their findings at a family reunion. It was your typical African American family reunion - a cookout held at a park, complete with matching T-shirts. It was here that I learned about my great-great-great-great-grandmother, an enslaved woman who lived on a Wake County plantation. Her name was Feely. I cried when I met her, seeing her name on the page before me. A name! I finally had a name to connect me to my past.

In 1833, Feely had a son, also born into slavery. His name was Rufus. At the age of 30, Rufus married his first wife, Etta. Together they had six children. Their daughter Mary, called Molly, was my great-great-grandmother. It is unknown to me who his father was, but she bore a son named Ned, or Edward. Edward married a woman named Maggie and had four children, including my grandfather, Robert Norris. Robert married Melba Walker. Together they had four children; one of them was my mother Brenda.

I was born Hope Lee Murdock, to Joe Murdock and Brenda Lee Murdock at 8:32 am on October 25th, 1974 at Norwegian American Hospital in Chicago, Illinois, a baby girl. This sentence alone carries so much. There is a record of my birth, my name, who my parents are, and where I was born. Mama Feely had none of that. No record of her birth, no documentation of her name, no indication of who her parents might have been. Disconnected. After finding Mama Feely's name at that family reunion, I felt a deep curiosity about who she might have been. My research journey began with a few sparse threads. The slave registers of 1850 and 1860 listed my enslaved family members by gender, age, and estimated value. But there were no names. My family's humanity was reduced to mere commodity. While these documents erased their identities, they also provided crucial clues.

Based on the records of her death date, I started piecing together her life timeline. Entries in those slave registries indicated that a woman of roughly the right age was owned by Samuel P. Norris, along with a boy who was more than likely Rufus. This surreal experience deepened when I found Feely listed by name in Norris's will, bequeathing her to his wife upon his death. My breath got really shallow when I read that. To see the complete lack of agency or bodily autonomy written in a legal document about one of my own family members still causes a feeling that is hard to name. Like a deep anxiety of being trapped or caged. But, I forced myself to take a deep breath and pressed on. In the various documents I uncovered, her name appeared as Febby, Feeby, and Feely—perhaps it was originally Phoebe. I have taken to calling her Mama Feely.

The definitive link between her and Rufus came when I found her name listed as his mother on the marriage certificate of Rufus and his second wife, Winnie. This discovery was a breakthrough, confirming that Mama Feely was indeed Rufus's mother. Each piece of information, from slave registries to marriage certificates, helped reconstruct the life of a woman whose origins had been systematically erased but whose legacy endures through our family's collective memory. That moment was a breakthrough. A sacred tether. She was real. She was mine.

Genealogy, Identity, and Healing: A Therapist's Reflection

As I've journeyed deeper into my own lineage, I've come to see that genealogy isn't just about names, dates, or dusty records. It's about healing. It's about restoring something that was broken. In therapeutic work, it's clear how identity formation is deeply tied to story. When people know where they come from, who their people were, how they lived, what they survived, it shapes how they see themselves in the present. And when those roots are missing, when there's no record or remembrance, it can leave a person feeling unmoored. Untethered. Like an orphan, even if they're surrounded by people.

Grief often shows up in those silences. Not always loud or obvious, but lingering. The grief of not knowing your grandmother's maiden name. The grief of not having a recipe passed down. The grief of holding questions that no one living can answer.

This is a kind of sorrow that doesn't always get named, but it lives in the body. It moves through generations. And often, it gets mistaken for personality: anxious, guarded, disconnected, overly independent, unsure. But underneath it? Sometimes there's just the ache of not knowing where you come from.

When a person finds even one ancestor—just one name, one story—it can begin to shift something deep within. Suddenly, that frame with no portrait inside starts to fill in. There is context for the resilience. There's evidence of survival. There's a reminder that life didn't begin with trauma, even if trauma tried to claim the story. There was something beautiful and rooted before the rupture.

Genealogy can be sacred work, especially for people descended from the transatlantic slave trade. It's not about romanticizing the past, it's about reclaiming what was stolen. It's about remembering that we come from a people who prayed, who built, who loved fiercely, who taught their children how to find joy even in chains. That remembering can be a form of protest. A kind of restoration. A quiet revolution of the soul.

When a person begins to unearth their ancestral story, it can create space for new narratives to form, narratives that affirm dignity, connection, and strength. The work is not always easy. Sometimes it's marked by dead ends and fragmented records. But even those fragments carry power. They speak. They echo. They remind us that we are part of something bigger than ourselves.

This is not just a historical project. It's a healing one.

Yes, Mama Feely is my 4x great-grandmother, an ancestor I "met" in 2016 at that family reunion through the pages of our family history book. However, here in this book, when I reference her, I am speaking of a real person, yet she also represents a composite of many women who were her contemporaries and who had come before her. Enslaved women. Women whose very existence hinged on the whims of another human being. Women who taught their children how to survive, how to have faith, and how to navigate the world they lived in with the lessons they themselves were taught as children.

Mama Feely serves as a guide and mentor throughout the book, offering wisdom and encouragement. When I think of her sharing this wisdom, I get the feelings one might associate with sitting between grandma's knees while she braids your hair, singing songs, and telling stories. I can smell something delicious in a pot on the stove or roasting in the oven. The air is warm, and she smells like shea butter and ivory soap. She is fat like me, and her thick legs are a comfortable place to lay my head. I think of being rooted, of belonging, of being anchored. I think of tenderness and care, but also strength and resilience.

I remember having a conversation with a friend about my journey of discovering my family history. As I described the process of uncovering names and stories of my ancestors, while she was fascinated and happy for me, she responded with a deep sadness. Like me before I began my journey, she, like most Americans descended from enslaved Africans, cannot trace their lineages back beyond great-grandparents if they're lucky. They don't have the names and places that help them understand who they are, why they are, and what their place is in this world. Seeing her pain, I invited her to be my "play cousin." Her response was one of extreme elation; she cried and thanked me for including her, grateful for the sense of connection and belonging. I get it. The pain of being disconnected is real.

Almost every Black person I know has "play" aunties and cousins, fictive kinship relationships that aren't based on blood or marriage but on close ties and mutual support. These bonds are formed through shared experiences, community, and a sense of solidarity. As previously stated, many Black people can't trace their lineage, so like I did for my friend, I offer to share mine. Y'all can be my "play cousins," OK? This book and the community we create can be like a perpetual St. Rocco's festival that tied my husband's people to Collelongo, their ancestral village in Italy. Join me on this journey as we create personal connections to the past, giving our history substance and forming relationships with those who have come before us. Perhaps my story, Mama Feely, and all she represents can be an anchor for you as well.

I feel like a griot, telling the story of our people and passing along lessons for the next generation.

In West African tradition, a griot is more than just a storyteller. Griots are oral historians, genealogists, musicians, praise-singers, poets, and community advisors all rolled into one. They are living libraries—keepers of memory—whose words don't just entertain, but preserve, instruct, and empower.

The role of the griot dates back centuries and is found most commonly among the Mandinka, Wolof, Fula, and other West African ethnic groups. Griots often belong to hereditary families, and their knowledge is passed down from generation to generation. They are trained to memorize complex histories, recite epics, and recall genealogies that can stretch back hundreds of years. Traditionally, griots use instruments like the *kora*, a 21-string lute-bridge-harp, or the *balafon*, a type of wooden xylophone, to accompany their performances, weaving rhythm and music into their narratives.

But griots are more than performers. They serve their communities as advisors, mediators, and preservers of moral and cultural values. Their words are binding, sacred even. To be called a griot is not merely a compliment—it is a calling.

For many African Americans, this tradition feels both familiar and faraway. We carry the spirit of the griot in our barbershop conversations, church testimonies, kitchen-table wisdom, and even our music. Yet we often do so without the full knowledge of the legacy we inherit. Reclaiming the griot spirit in our work, especially in the work of healing, is a way to honor both our ancestors and the future we are shaping with our words. As Thomas Hale says in *Griots and Griottes: Masters of Words and Music*, "The griot's role is not just to repeat history, but to shape it, to make it live again in each generation. Their work is deeply communal and spiritual."

Though I feel like a griot, talking about me *being* a griot makes me uncomfortable. I am so disconnected from my African-ness. I don't know the protocol. I don't know how to engage, so at the risk of being offensive to my African cousins, I ask for grace. like many things in African American culture, I have to be innovative, filling in the gaps with new things while trying to weave together what I know from experience and what was handed down to me. That's what we do. We make do, and we get through, and we make something new - like jazz music and soul food.

In exploring my family's past, I discovered that Feely was more than just a name on a page. She represented resilience, strength, and survival. Her story became a bridge to my own sense of identity and belonging. Feely's son, Rufus, was born into slavery in 1833. Despite the odds, he was freed in 1856 and went on to amass significant land holdings, a testament to his perseverance and ingenuity. His daughter, Mary, continued this legacy of resilience, passing it down through generations to my grandfather, Robert Norris, and eventually to me.

The journey to uncover these stories was not easy. It involved sifting through historical records, piecing together fragmented narratives, and often relying on oral histories passed down through family members. But each discovery, each name, and each story added a new layer to my understanding of who I am and where I come from.

One of the interesting moments in this journey was discovering the concept of Ubuntu. Ubuntu is a Nguni Bantu term meaning "humanity." It is often translated as "I am because we are," emphasizing the interconnectedness of all people. This philosophy stands in stark contrast to the ideas of rugged individualism and manifest destiny that have shaped much of American history. In the context of African American culture, Ubuntu manifests in the strong sense of community and kinship that binds us together, even in the face of adversity.

As I delved deeper into my family's history, I realized that the values of Ubuntu were woven into the very fabric of African American culture. Our ancestors, despite the brutal conditions of slavery, found ways to support and care for one another. They created networks of fictive kinship, forming bonds that went beyond blood relations. This sense of community and mutual support has been part of the fabric of African American culture and has played a crucial role in our survival and resilience.

Mama Feely embodies these values. She is not just a figure from the past but a symbol of the strength, wisdom, and love that have been passed down through generations. When I think of her, I envision a matriarch who provides comfort and guidance. Her presence in this book is meant to offer that same sense of comfort and guidance to my readers.

As I stand today, I am no longer an orphan but a griot, a storyteller and keeper of my family's history. I carry the weight and wisdom of my ancestors, and it is both an honor and my duty to pass these stories on to future generations. In doing so, I honor their struggles, their triumphs, and their enduring legacy.

Reflecting on my journey, I am reminded of a meme I saw on social media about ancestor math. It stated that in order to be born, you need: 2 parents, 4 grandparents, 8 great-grandparents, 16 second great-grandparents, 32 third great-grandparents, 64 fourth great-grandparents, 128 fifth great-grandparents, 256 sixth great-grandparents, 512 seventh great-grandparents, 1,024 eighth great-grandparents, and 2,048 ninth great-grandparents. For you to be born today from 12 previous generations, you needed a total of 4,096 ancestors over the last 400 years. Just think about their struggles, battles, difficulties, sadness, happiness, and love stories. How many expressions of hope for the future? How much did they have to undergo for you to exist in this present moment?

This underscores the importance of knowing and honoring our ancestors. Each one of those 4,096 individuals contributed to my existence, and their stories are a part of my story. By embracing this heritage, I am not only connecting with my past but also ensuring that the legacy of my ancestors continues to live on.

I invite you to embark on your own path of discovery. Whether you can trace your lineage back centuries or only know a few of your relatives' names, recognizing and embracing your roots is a powerful step toward healing. This exploration is not just about personal growth; it's a proactive step against systemic racism and the maladaptive behaviors that stem from intergenerational racialized trauma. Remember, you are a person crafted in the image of the Creator, designed with purpose and inherent dignity. This book aims to serve as a guide, offering stories, wisdom, and a sense of community to all who seek to understand their place in this grand design. As we validate our humanity, we not only acknowledge ourselves as worthy, but also honor God and His goodness. In a later chapter, we will delve deeper into the concept of *Imago Dei*, the image of God in each of us, setting the foundation for a transformative understanding of our individual and collective identities and combating the impacts of historical injustices.

Now let's go deeper. Let's go back to the origin story of racialized trauma for Americans descended from enslaved Africans. OK, I can already hear the resistance of wondering why we always have to talk about when our people were slaves and how bad it was. But Sis, I'm not inviting you on this journey so that we can retraumatize ourselves, but so that we can be clear-eyed. What if what we believe is personality or culture are actually trauma responses decontextualized over time? This dive into history is an attempt to offer context. To show what's what.

CHAPTER 3

Reckoning

It's dark. Cold. A tapping sound wakes me from a restless sleep. I open my eyes to find myself in a dim, unfamiliar room. The coldness wraps around me, and the confusion settles in my chest. It's a feeling I know all too well, like the fog I sometimes wake up with in real life. That disoriented sense of not knowing where you are or how you got there, that's trauma's fingerprint. It blurs the lines between past and present, sleep and waking, memory and reality. Wooden walls surround me—rough-hewn logs sealed with chinking. My heart races. Where am I? Why am I here?

The tapping gets louder, insistent. I rise from a low wooden cot and cross the hard-packed dirt floor. My bare feet feel the chill. I lift the heavy crossbar from the door and pull it open.

An old woman stands there, holding a flickering oil lamp. Her eyes are deep and knowing. I recognize her somehow. Her face reminds me of my own reflection. I pause, caught between surprise and something close to fear.

"Come on here wit' me, girl. Mama Feely gots things to show you," she says, her voice like a thread of history, pulling me in. Her free hand grips mine, firm and determined. There's no going back now.

We walk along a narrow path under the cover of night. The air feels heavy with the weight of truth unspoken. My feet crunch on leaves and twigs. The ground is uneven. I wince as a sharp rock presses into my heel.

"Mama Feely, I need to go back. I need shoes... a jacket," I say. But she doesn't stop.

"Dis walk ain't meant to be con'table, chile. You don' dress up fo' de truth. You face it. Head on. Barefoot if you gots to."

Every step is a reminder: this journey isn't about comfort—it's about clarity. The kind that pricks and pierces like the rocks beneath my feet.

Mama Feely glances at me, her voice gentler now.

"You been feelin' off, ain't you? Like you don't got no patience no mo'. Like you always on edge, snappin' at folks or pullin' away when you don' mean to. Or some days, you jes heavy for no reason at all—cain't get up, cain't stop de tears, cain't find your joy."

She pauses, eyes searching mine.

"Dat ain't jus' moods, baby. Dat's somethin' dat done settle in yo' bones. It live in de body when de soul been carryin' too much for too long. And de hard part? It don' always come from *yo'* life. Some o' that weight? It's old. It belonged to de ones who came befo' you."

She leaned in, her hands folded like she was cradling something precious.

"Our people been carryin' burdens since b'fo' dey set foot on dis here and. Hurt dat ain't got no name. Tears dat never got to fall. We had to keep goin'. Had to be strong, even when we was breakin' inside. And all dat pain? It didn' jus' vanish. It

49

made a home in our blood. Got passed down like a family recipe, 'cept dis one don' feed nobody. It just weigh you down."

She took a breath, slow and deep, then looked me square in the eye.

"But baby, jus' 'cause it came wit you don't mean it gotta stay wit you."

She reached up, tapping her chest.

"You got de power to name it, r'lease it, give it back to God. You don' have to carry what your mama carried, or your grandmama, or de ones befo' her. Dey did what dey had to do so *you* could have a chance to do somethin' diff'rent. Dat don't mean forgettin' 'em. It mean *honorin'* 'em. By livin'. By healin'. By tellin' the truth."

She smiled then, soft but sure.

"Truth is, baby, you was never meant to do this alone. De same God dat kept dem is still keepin' you. De same Spirit dat whispered to dem in hush harbors can still bring peace to yo' mind right now today."

She squeezes my hand. "And now? We reckonin' wit it, together."

She placed a hand over her heart and let the silence settle, like a prayer in the dark.

Then, with a deep breath, she turned, reaching for the oil lamp.

"Come on, now," she said, her voice steady. "dere's somethin' else you need to know if'n you gon' heal right. Truth got buried deep—but we gon' dig it up."

She raises the lamp as we step forward, the light casting long shadows as we approach a clearing.

"Dere was a time when folks wasn't called 'Black' or 'White.' Naw, baby. Dat mess came later. Wasn't God who made dat divide—it was man. Power an' greed turned us into separate camps. Turned kinfolk into strangers. I'm gon' tell ya 'bout John Punch, Elizabeth Key, and how de ones in charge twist de laws to split us. Made it so skin color d'cided your worth—not 'cause it was natural, but 'cause it kept 'em rich."

I nod, though the truth sinks slow—heavy like wet soil.
It's more than history. It's personal.

Because what they did back then?
I still feel it now.

The Virginia Company

The Virginia Company of London. A business venture dressed up like a noble cause. In 1606, the British Crown handed them a sweeping land grant—everything from the edges of western New York down through the Carolinas, stretching westward all the way to the Mississippi River. Timber, rivers, fertile soil, wild game. It was a fortune waiting to be extracted. And the men behind it? They weren't looking to settle, they were looking to dominate.

They saw the land as untapped wealth. Raw, ripe, and ready. But of course, it wasn't empty. Entire nations of people already lived here, people with languages, systems of governance, spirituality, trade, and community. But to the Englishmen, they didn't count. They weren't Christians, and in the twisted logic of the British Empire, that meant they weren't fully human.

Colonial greed doesn't see neighbors—it sees obstacles.
And when profit is the goal, conscience is often the first casualty.

I read the charter of the Virginia Company in the preparation for writing this book. The audacity is appalling.

"We would vouchsafe unto them our licence, to make habitation, plantation, and to deduce a colony of sundry of our people into that part of America commonly called Virginia, and other parts and territories in America, either appertaining unto us, or which are not now actually possessed by any christian prince or people,...

III. We greatly commending, and graciously accepting of, their desires for the furtherance of so noble a work, which may, by the providence of Almighty God, hereafter tend to the glory of his divine Majesty, in propagating of Christian religion to such people, as yet live in darkness and miserable ignorance of the true knowledge and worship of God, and may in time bring the infidels and savages, living in those parts, to human civility, and to a settled and quiet government; "

So the colonizers justified displacement with scripture and law, wrapping conquest in the language of "civilizing missions" and divine right. This is the made up theological alibi that made extraction feel righteous. Indigenous people became a problem to be removed. And soon, Africans would become a solution to be exploited. Both dehumanized. Both commodified. Because the system they were building wasn't about justice or liberty—it was about control. And profit. Always profit.

"It was de love o' money," Mama Feely says, her voice tight, like the words hurt to speak. "Ain't dat what de Good Book say? *De love of money is de root of all kind of evil.* And baby, dey proved it. Dey was tryin' to 'rase folks from de earth. Like they ain't never been here in de firs' place. Slavery, stealin' land—all in de name o' profit. Folks built fortunes off o' blood, an' called it blessed."

We walk in silence for a while. The woods around us seem to lean in, wind rustling like memory.

"But it wasn't just de takin' dat cut deep," she says softly. "It was the *strippin'.* They didn't just steal land or labor—dey stole *dignity.* Made our people feel like nothin'. Like we ain't got no heart. No soul. No mind worth listenin' to. Dat's how dey held power—by tryin' to grind us down, break our spirit so bad we forget who we was."

She stops and looks at me, steady and sure.
"But we didn' forget. Not all de way. And dat's why we still here."

We stop at an old cabin, its wooden walls sagging under the weight of time.

"Dis de place," Mama Feely says, raising her lamp. "Dis where dey firs' brought us."

She doesn't rush her words. Each one drops like a stone in a still pond.

"Back in 1619, some Englishmen—privateers, dey called 'em, but pirates is what dey really was—stole near fifty Angola people off a Portuguese ship call' St. John de Baptist. Can you b'lieve dat name? Folks already snatched from home once. And now taken again. Only twenty-somethin' made it though. Brought 'em right here to a place called Jamestown. No kin. No tongue dey could understand. Just sorrow in dey bones an' salt in dey wounds."

I shiver—not from the cold, but from the weight of it.

Mama Feely's voice lowers, her eyes dim with memory that don't belong to her but lives in her just the same.

"Ain't long after dat, 'round 1640, dere was a man name John Punch. He tried to run—just wanted to be free. Took off wit two white fellas who was indentured like him. Dey got caught. All three. But you know what? Those white mens jus' got more years tacked on to dey contract. John? Dey chained dat man fo' life."

She pauses. Lets it hang there like smoke.

"Same crime. Diff'rent skin. Dat's when dey started makin' de lines real clear."

I stop in my tracks. My chest tightens.

A man thrown into slavery not for what he did—but for who he was. Virginia's council sentenced Punch to lifetime servitude while his European counterparts received term extensions, marking one of the earliest documented instances in the colony where African descent determined a harsher, inheritable condition..
I thought I knew American history. But this? This is definitely not the version they taught us in school. I think of all the times I've been treated different and told I was imagining it.

This wasn't new.

This was old.

Older than I ever knew.

She lets the silence hold that truth.

Mama Feely walks slow, eyes on the ground like she's listening for something under the soil.

"Den come Elizabeth Key," she says, her voice steady but sharp. "It was 1656. Her mama was African, A slave. But her daddy? White. A man wit land an' power. Now, Elizabeth, she had to *fight* in court jus' to be recognized as free. And she won! But not 'cause justice was just. She won 'cause her daddy was a white Christian. Dat's what saved her."

I clenched my fists, heat rising in my throat.
So, at that time, freedom had a back door—and you needed whiteness, or the approval of a white man, to slip through it.

Mama Feely stops and turns to me. Her eyes catch the light from the lamp, glowing like coals in the dark.
"It warn't 'bout what was right. It was 'bout keepin' power where dey wanted it."

We keep walking. A chilly wind picks up, but the stories? They're hot on my skin.

"Den came 1662 seven years later," she says. "Dat's when dey passed a law—*partus sequitur ventrem*. Fancy Latin, but it mean dis: a child would follow de condition of de mother. So even if your daddy was free, if your mama was a slave—you was, too."

I swallowed hard. That law sealed it. Before the passing of this law the colony operated under English common law that stated that children inherited the social and legal status of their father. And with so many slave owners producing children with enslaved women, they could have a problem. So they didn't just chain our bodies—they chained our babies before they ever took a breath.

They made the wombs of enslaved women into cages. Wrote bondage into bloodlines. It wasn't just cruelty, it was economic policy. And it worked exactly how they meant it to.

My stomach tightens. I feel it. The cage forming.

"Bacon's Rebellion," Mama Feely says, her tone dropping like a stone in a well. "1676. Po' white folks an' Black folks rose up together. Dey saw what was really goin' on—it warn't 'bout skin, it was 'bout power. Dey was tired. Tired of bein' used. Tired of bein' hungry while de rich got fat off they backs."

She shakes her head, slow.

"But when dat rebellion failed? Whew. De folks in charge got *scared*. Real scared. Said, 'Dis cain't happen again. So dey came up wit a plan."

She leans in, her voice a near-whisper.

"Dey start handin' po' folks from Europe jus' enough—crumbs, really. A lil' land here. A title dere. Called 'em 'better than de Negro.' Gave 'em a sliver of status so they'd guard de gates dat held us captive."

My voice is barely audible. "They invented racism. Turned it into a weapon." After Bacon's Rebellion rattled Virginia's ruling class, the colony's leaders started handing out crumbs to poor whites. Not to truly lift them, but to keep them from uniting again with Black laborers. These crumbs looked like tax breaks, the right to bear arms in the militia, or even small parcels of land on the frontier. Each policy drew a sharper color line, teaching poor whites that their loyalty, and their sense of status, came from being 'not Black.'

"Mmmhmm," she hums. "Dat's right, baby. It warn't born outta hate. It was born outta *strategy*. By 1705, dey done wrote it down in law—said no Negro, mulatto, or Indian could buy no Christian servant, 'less they looked like 'em. See what that mean, baby? Even if'n you was free, even if'n you found Jesus, dey still made sure whiteness stayed up top. Freedom had a fence 'round it if your skin was dark. The hate? That came later—after the system got good and settle in."

We reach the edge of a small field. The moon overhead peeks through the clouds, soft and watchful.

Mama Feely slows her steps, and her words take on an old, rhythmic cadence—like a sermon, like a lullaby made of truth.

"Dey kept changin' de laws to keep us apart. Gave poor white folks a seat at de table—just not de feast. Made 'em feel rich just 'cause dey wasn't Black. And that? Dat was de start o' de lie."

57

She turns to me, steady and sure.

"De lie dat whiteness mean you was some*body*. And Blackness? Dat mean you was some*thing*. Somethin' to be owned, bridled, or worked."

To keep the rest of us low and fighting each other instead of the real enemy. It was never about color—it was always about control.

And we've been living in the aftermath ever since.

"Dat's how dey did it, chile," Mama Feely says, lifting the lamp, her face glowing with sorrow and fire. "Took 'em over a hundred years—law by law, lie by lie—to try and break us down on purpose. All 'cause of de evil dat come from de love o' money." She paused then took my hand, "And dat weight you carry? That grief, that rage, that feelin' like you don't belong? Baby, that ain't just yours. It been passed down like hand-me-down sorrow. But listen close—it don't stop here. Dis *ain't* de end of your story."

She stops and looks at me, the light flickering between us.

"You ever wonder why yo' heart race when your boss wanna talk to you? Why your stomach twistin' before you even see him? Why you always waitin' fo' somethin' bad to happen, even when thangs look calm?"

I nod, slowly.

Because yes. I *have* wondered.

"Dat's 'cause trauma got memory, baby," she says, her voice low and full of knowing. "It don't forget. It jus' goe quiet, hides in de corners of your body—till somethin' calls it up. That ain't you bein' weak. That's you carryin' more than what's visible."

Her words settle into me like a weight and a balm, all at once. The body I inhabit in 2025 learned lessons codified in 1705.

I think about the moments I've felt like I couldn't breathe, and didn't know why.

The way my shoulders tense when I hear a sudden noise.

The way I brace for rejection, even in rooms where I should feel safe.

It's not imagination.

It's not oversensitivity.

It's memory.

Body memory.

Passed through blood, shaped by survival.

And in that moment, I know:

I'm not crazy.

I'm not broken.

I am carrying generations of survival in my bones. In systems designed for my subjugation.

Mama Feely smiles, soft but strong.

"We got heart, chile. We got soul. We got fight. And we *rise.*

That's why we walk this path—

To understand.

To remember.

To heal."

I nod. Tears sting my eyes. But I'm awake. Fully awake. And with every step, I know I'm not walking just for me. I'm walking for them. And for what's still to come.

As we near the end of the path, Mama Feely stops. Her eyes hold the weight of generations—and a glimmer of strength.

"Now you see, baby, how dey set the stage. The greed, de division, de laws—dey all worked together. But dis? Dis is jus' de beginnin'. What come next... it was darker still. When dey made us property, when dey took not jus' our freedom but tried to take our very humanity—dat's when de real battle began."

She takes a deep breath. "What we talkin' 'bout now is American chattel slav'ry. De kind dat warn't jus' 'bout labor—it was 'bout ownership of bodies, hearts, and dreams."

The air grows still.

"Come on, chile. Dere's more to see. You ready to learn 'bout de cost? De cost of all dey took from us—an' de price we paid to hold onto our spirits?"

She steps forward. The lamp flickers. Her shadow stretches long into the darkness.

And now, dear reader, we pause.

Because this isn't just history—it's a wound still open.

The society the colonizers set up wasn't just rooted in economic ambition—it was built on deliberate division. They didn't simply enslave bodies; they engineered systems to fracture communities, pit neighbor against neighbor, and normalize the dehumanization of an entire people. That system never truly ended—it just evolved.

As a therapist, I see how those roots still bear bitter fruit.

You might feel that sting when your heart races after a microaggression you try to shrug off, like a backhanded compliment about how good at basketball your tall 11 year old son must be. Nevermind that he hates sports and loves building robots. When you brace yourself before walking into a room where you're the only one who looks like you. When you overthink your tone in emails or swallow your frustration to stay "professional."

That's survival. That's your nervous system doing its best to protect you in a world still shaped by the hierarchy that colonial capitalism birthed. For generations, our people have had to learn the art of vigilance—and of shape-shifting to stay safe.

And while those strategies helped our ancestors make it through, they come with a cost: chronic stress, anxiety, depression, dissociation, a deep sense of disconnection from ourselves and one another. What you're feeling isn't personal failure—it's a collective inheritance.

But here's the thing about inheritance: once we name it, we can decide what to keep and what to release. We can grieve the harm, honor the strength, and build new patterns rooted in dignity and connection.

So if you're feeling heavy, please know: that heaviness makes sense. You are remembering. And healing starts by telling the truth—just like Mama Feely said.

Let's keep walking.

Mama Feely pauses before taking that next step. She turns to me once more, then closes her eyes and whispers a prayer that sinks into the soil beneath us and rises up into the stars above.

"Lord, walk wit us through dis truth. Give dis child strength fo' de reckonin' and courage for de healin'. Let her 'member dat she come from warriors, from wisdom, from worth. Let what's been hidden come to light, an' let dat light set her free."

She opens her eyes and nods. "Truth ain't here to harm you, baby. It's here to heal you. It might sting at first, but it's de start of your freedom."

She steps forward. The lamp flickers. Her shadow stretches long into the darkness.

CHAPTER 4

American Chattel Slavery
The Cost of Capitalism and the Human Spirit

The woods opened up to a quiet clearing, and there it was—the little cabin where this journey began.

The door creaked open, welcoming us into the hush of something ancestral and familiar. The hearth was already warm, flames crackling low and steady. Mama Feely moved like she'd never left this plane of existence. Like she belonged here in this space, to the fire in the hearth, and to the healing I knew was in the pots on the stove.

She reached for the kettle, now steaming, and poured water over fresh mint leaves we'd gathered along the path. The smell was sharp, grounding—alive. "Go on, now," she said, handing me a chipped mug. "Dis'll settle your spirit. You gon' need it."

We sat at her kitchen table, a slab of wood worn smooth by years of elbows, plates of good food, laughter, and tears. It was the kind of table where truth got told—not always easy, but always necessary. The kind of table where women gathered to gossip, grieve and get free.

Mama Feely ran her fingers along the grain, tracing invisible lines as if she could touch the memories etched in wood.

"Dey say it was jus' business,' but chile, let me tell you somethin'—when you put money above mercy, you lose your soul."

She looked up, steady.

"Don't let nobody fool you, baby. Slav'ry warn't jus' 'bout work—it was 'bout wealth. 'Bout makin' men rich, no matter de cost. Greed so deep it crossed oceans an' swallered up whole nations like dey was nothin'.

Them folks dey call saltwater Negroes—de ones fresh off'n de ships from Africa? Dey ain't see 'em as people. Naw. Dey saw strong backs, good teeth, an' a price tag. Tore families apart. Packed God's children into boats like cargo. And when they got here? Wrote 'em down in ledgers, sold 'em off like furniture, counted 'em like crops."

She shakes her head, eyes low.

"Dat's what this country was built on—not freedom, baby. Fortune."

She didn't shout. She didn't have to.

"But don't get your thinkin' tangled up now," she says, her voice firm like she was setting the record straight. "Dey didn't just steal labor—dey tried to steal everything. Stole lullabies outta mamas' mouths. Stole land our people never got back. Stole names we ain't even know we lost. Took babies right out they mama's arms like it was nothin'.Dey ain't just chain up our bodies, baby. Dey tried to wipe out our soul. Tried to make us forget who we was—who we still is."

She paused. Sipped her tea. The fire cracked again.

A Child Torn from Her Mother

Mama Feely's gaze drifted toward the window. Her voice thinned to a whisper.

"I was 'bout six years old the day dey sold me. Samuel P. Norris. Dat was his name. I 'member de boots he wore—mud still clingin' to de heels. My mama. Lord, my mama held me so tight I couldn't breathe. Told me, 'Don't cry, baby. Be brave.'

But I cried anyway. Screamed when dey pulled me offa her. Clawed at her dress 'til I tore it."

She went quiet.

"He checked my teeth. My arms. Said I was 'strong for a lil' one.' Called me an investment as he picked me up and put me in dat wagon. I didn't know what dat meant. I jus' knew Mama was gettin' smaller an smaller behind me. And den she was gone."

She touched her chest.

"Folks say chillun forget. But our bodies remember. Dat cry, it lived in me long after her voice faded. De pain was wit me even in my sleep. I kept wakin' up reachin' fo' her, even after I couldn't 'member her face no mo'. Dat's what pain like that do. It don't jus' hurt your heart, it mark you. Like fingerprints pressed deep in yo' flesh."

She looked at me hard, but tender.

"Dat's why sometimes you cry an' don't know why. Why you feel heavy fo' no reason. You might be carryin' grief that ain't yours but still live in you."

The Economics of Flesh

She sat back in her chair, hands resting on the table's edge.

"Slav'ry was a system dat made dey whole way o' life work. A machine made of Black backs and powerful people's greed. Cotton, sugar, rice, tobacco—all planted in blood-soaked ground. Black folks weren't seen as people. We was inventory. Assets. Breedin' stock."

I took it all in and said to myself, And still… the Spirit of the people lived.

"I keep sayin' it, 'cause its true. De love of money is de root of all kind of evil. And evil'll make a man forget dat every soul is made in the image of God."

She looked toward the door.

"Come on now. Come in, daughters. The table is open."

The door creaked as four women stepped into the room, their faces creased with memory, their backs straight with dignity. They did not ask permission. They took their place like they belonged. Because they did.

Mama Feely nodded. "Tell it like it was. We ready."

Louisa Adams leaned forward first, hands folded tight.

"My missus wuz kind to me, but Mars Tom wuz the buger… Lawd, you better not be caught wid a book in yor han'. If you did, you were sold. Dey didn't 'low dat."

She shook her head, eyes glistening. "Dere wuz no church on the plantation, and we were not lowed to have prayer meetin's… no parties, no dances. No sir. You

66

couldn't travel without a pass. And de pateroller? They were always watchin'. Nighttime wasn't never safe."

The room went still. Mama Feely reached over and touched her hand.

"You here now, baby. You seen it and you told it. That matter."

Ida Adkins took her turn next, her voice sharp and tired.

"My mammy an' pappy belonged to Marse Frank. He worked 'em hard on half rations. Said he was good to us, but good don't feed no belly. We was always hungry."

She looked around the room, then directly at me.

"They ain't never beat us too bad, but don't let nobody tell you hunger ain't a whip."

Martha Allen spoke up, her words thick with hurt and fury.

"I'se hyard mammy say they went ter wuck widout breakfast. When she left her baby in the kitchen, she'd drink from the slop bucket jus' to keep goin'. Young marster wanted her bad, but she said no—so he hit her on the head with a lightwood knot."

Her voice cracked.

"That's how they punished you for sayin' no. That's how they made babies with women they owned."

She looked straight into the fire.

"My daddy's daddy was one of 'em. One o' them Carpet Gitters they was called."

Mama Feely nodded slowly.

"Truth like that don't rot—it reveals."

Finally, Sarah Louise Augustus stood. Her voice was soft, but every syllable cut like a blade.

"I wus born on a plantation near Fayetteville. When a slave was no good, they sold 'em on the block in the center of the street."

She paused. And in that silence, a cold realization washed over me.

I've lived in North Carolina since the early 1990s. The city of Fayetteville was familiar to me. I'd driven those streets,even passed by that building a time or two. The city's logo—until 2015—was the slave market house she just mentioned. The same one that still stands in the center of town.

It's hard to fathom. The callousness. The indifference. The way some folks can treat a site of horror like it's just another piece of local history. A landmark. A logo.

It wasn't just tone deaf—it was a refusal to reckon.

"I seen 'em whip men till they skin come off. Seen 'em hang folks on Ramsey Street at exactly noon. I was just a child. I ran off once—just to see a man get hung. That's how common death was. That's what they raised us on."

The fire cracked sharply.

"My grandma," she added, "was a healer. Wet-nursed all the white babies, even after freedom. Cured folks of rheumatism with hops and herbs."4

Mama Feely bowed her head.

"She carried life even while they carried death."

"We honor every word you spoke," I said softly. "You're not forgotten. Not here. Not anymore."

Mama Feely looked at each of them, eyes shining. Then she stood slowly and walked to the hearth, her back to us, her voice low.

"You know what happens to a people when they live like this for too long? When they watch they mama sold off, they brother beaten bloody, they babies buried in silence?"

She turned, eyes glinting with firelight.

"It don't just disappear after freedom come.Naw, baby. Hurt like that? It shape folks—shape how they walk, how they love, how they raise they babies. Whether it was right or not, that pain got stitched into every generation, neat as a hem. Passed down like a quilt soaked in sorrow—right on down to you."

She looked around at the women seated at the table—Louisa, Ida, Martha, Sarah Louise—and then at me.

"This ain't just history. It's a rancid inheritance."

She came back to the table and pressed her palm flat against the wood.

"When a whole people is treated like property—bought and sold like a stew pot or a sack o' feed—you best believe it show up later. It show up when folks don't know how to stay. When daddies disappear 'cause they never got to be protectors. When mamas gotta be tough and tender all at once 'cause they know this world chew up Black babies fast."

Her throat caught for a second, but she kept on..

"When a woman cain't say no without fear in her bones. When a child grow up wit no mama or papa, never hearin' 'I love you,' 'cause nobody never said it to the peoples dat was raisin' them up neither."

She turned to me now.

"And when folks been fed on half rations, you learn to fight over scraps—but you also learn how to hide your rebellion. They called us lazy, slow, stupid. But they ain't see the brilliance in that resistance. Walkin' slow in them fields, takin' our time, breakin' tools by 'accident'? Baby, that was rebellion in rags. That was genius in disguise.

She turned her gaze toward Sarah Louise.

"And when women like her grandmama was mixin' herbs and roots into teas and tonics—not just to heal, but to keep from bringin' another soul into slav'ry—dat was resistance, too. But dey ain't call it that. Called us witches, called it superstition. But the truth is, we was scientists. Midwives. Freedom fighters in aprons an' headwraps."

She leaned back, shaking her head soft.

"But over time some o' us f'got dat. We swallowed dey stories. Started believing de lie dat we was de problem."

She touched her own chest. Then she looked back at the women.

"They ain't jus' tellin' what happened. They showin' us where the wound got made. So we can stop pretendin' de hurt parts of us is just broke for no reason."

I felt something shift in my bones. Not just understanding—permission. To feel, to question, to grieve. To trace the bruise beneath the skin and name it for what it was. Because what was Mama Feely saying? It echoed what trauma therapist Dr. Resmaa Menakem says about trauma decontextualized over time. Because what they called laziness, stupidity, or superstition? That wasn't brokenness. That was survival— misunderstood, misnamed, and passed down without context. But now, we're putting the context back in. We're remembering the why behind the wounds.

"Y'all done poured truth into this house." Mama Feely told the ladies around the table. "Go on an' rest now. We got it from here."

They nodded, one by one, and made their way to the door. Their presence didn't leave though—it settled into the walls, into the air.

"Come on, baby," Mama Feely said, sitting back down in her chair. "Let's see who else gone visit."

I sat there after the women had gone, after Mama Feely's words settled into the grain of the table. The fire was still warm, but something colder pressed at the edges of my heart.

Because here's the thing...

What we just heard?

It wasn't just their trauma. As individuals descended from enslaved Africans, it lives in us, too. I'm not saying that every pain they carried is ours to carry too. Not every wound is our wound. But still - something lingers. There's a weight that settles in the body, even when we can't name it. A quiet echo that humms through the bloodline. And when we listen close, when we stop long enough to feel, it becomes clear. Because those same systems, that hunger for profit at any human cost didn't die with emancipation—it just changed uniforms. It's still with us today, in underpaid labor, in healthcare gaps, in prison cells.

You ever wonder why some of us work ourselves to the bone—doing the most, carrying it all—yet still feel like it's not enough? Like no matter how much we give, we still owe more?

Maybe it's not just personality or pressure.

Maybe it's inheritance.

I think about how my mom used to say to my brother and I, "That school better not call me while I'm at work." Not because she didn't care—but because labor, productivity, and keeping her job came first. She knew what it cost to be seen as a problem, especially on the job. She couldn't afford softness—not at work, and sometimes, not even at home.

And that's not just her. That's so many of us.

Why do some families go quiet when emotions rise? Like saying too much might shatter the room?

Why do we flinch when we're praised? Shut down when there's conflict?

Why do we push love away—right when it's trying to reach us?

These aren't random quirks. They're patterns—passed down, learned through struggle, etched into our nervous systems by generations who had to survive first and feel later. What may have started as necessary coping skills—like staying silent to stay safe, suppressing emotion, bracing for danger that might never come, always being ready to fight, to run, or to please—once kept our ancestors alive. But over time, as each generation learned from the last, those same survival strategies began to settle in as habits. And now? What once protected us may be holding us back.

A rancid inheritance.

We were never meant to carry the weight of being considered property. Neither were our ancestors, but somehow they did. They carried it on their backs, in their wombs, in their blood.

And because trauma doesn't just disappear, they passed down not only their strength that helped them survive—but also their scars.

As a therapist, I've seen it over and over again. Trauma that isn't healed doesn't just sit still—it gets passed down.

So, what can happen to a people when they're dehumanized by systems, bought and sold for generations? Again, not everything I mention will apply to everyone, but here are some things for your consideration.

Attachment Wounds

Our ancestors knew love. They knew belonging and kinship. But slavery disrupted the most sacred bond between mother and child, parent and family. Children were sold off like livestock—no time for goodbye, no control over what happened next. Mothers grieved babies they could never find again. Fathers were denied the right to protect or raise their children. Whole families lived with the knowledge that someone they loved could be taken at any moment.

And now?

That legacy still echoes in the quiet spaces of our relationships. It shows up when we fear people will leave us without warning. When we get close to someone, but something inside us pulls back—just in case they disappear. It shows up when we struggle to trust our partners, our friends, even ourselves. When we parent our own children with a mix of fierce love and deep anxiety, always bracing for something to go wrong.

Could it be that it's not that we don't want love? It's that our blood remembers what it felt like to lose it.

Educational Barriers

Reading was illegal for many of our ancestors. Let that settle in.

To learn was to risk your life. To teach another Black person to read was an act of rebellion. The ability to interpret words, to write your name, to sign a document—that was power, and the system knew it.

How might this show up today? It shows up when a Black child is labeled "behind" in school and internalizes it as "I'm not smart." It shows up when we feel shame asking for help, or freeze in academic spaces, or avoid paperwork, or dread parent-teacher conferences—not because we're lazy or indifferent, but because somewhere along the line, learning got tied to something dangerous.

Many of us are still unlearning that lie—that we're not enough.

We are enough. We've always been enough. And we are reclaiming what was once stolen: our right to know, to question, to grow, to make space for our brilliance.

Control and Obedience

Under slavery, survival often depended on how well you could read a room, keep your head down, and stay out of the way. Speaking out could get you whipped. Making eye contact could be seen as "disrespect." Joy, defiance, or simply existing too boldly could cost you everything.

So our ancestors adapted. They became careful. Quiet. Sharp observers. They learned to shrink around certain people or groups, to code-switch, to make themselves smaller to stay safe.

Fast forward to now, and many of us are still living in those patterns—over-apologizing, people-pleasing, saying "yes" when our bodies are screaming "no." We feel guilty for taking naps, hesitant to ask for what we need, unsure if we're allowed to rest, be seen, or take up space.

But survival isn't the same as freedom.

Our ancestors paid the price for our safety. Now we get to ask: What would it mean to live without always shrinking?

Physical Illness and Chronic Stress

Slavery wasn't just psychological violence—it was physical terrorism. The constant threat of beatings, starvation, rape, and death placed Black bodies in an unrelenting state of fear. And fear, when it's prolonged, doesn't just stay in the mind—it rewires the body.

Today, if that inherited stress response still lives in us. It can look like:

Constant Vigilance, Even When Nothing Is Wrong

You might know this feeling: your body's on high alert, even in peaceful settings. You're always scanning—consciously or not—for what might go wrong. You listen for tone shifts in people's voices. You monitor body language in every room. You keep a backup plan on deck, even at church or brunch.

That's not paranoia. It's your nervous system doing exactly what it was trained to do—to survive.

For generations, Black folks have had to read the world for danger. Not just physical danger, but emotional, racial, and economic harm. Vigilance kept us alive. But it also wears us down. Constant scanning burns energy we don't realize we're using, leaving us depleted and on edge, even in rest.

Startling Easily

If you jump at sudden noises, flinch when someone enters a room unannounced, or feel your chest tighten when someone raises their voice—even if you know they mean no harm—your body is responding to perceived threat.

This is not weakness, or even quirkyness. It's hyperarousal. When trauma teaches the nervous system that the world isn't safe, it can become like a sensitive smoke alarm—triggered quickly, hard to calm down.

Our ancestors lived with real, constant threats—threats that were built into the laws, the culture, the very soil of this country. And today, that same wiring might still be firing inside you. Because let's be honest: the danger didn't disappear. It just changed shape. That's why we still see arrests for "driving while Black." Why we still hold our breath during traffic stops or when our child runs out the door in a hoodie.

But here's the grace:

You can learn to reset the alarm system.

Gently.

Patiently.

With love.

Your body may remember the fear—but it can also learn what safety feels like. We'll get to that later.

Trouble Sleeping

Sleep is supposed to be a place of rest. But for many of us, night is when our minds race, our hearts pound, and our bodies feel the least safe. Falling asleep may take forever. Staying asleep may feel impossible.

For people descended from those who had to wake before dawn to avoid punishment—or be on guard against violence in the night—rest doesn't always feel safe. That trauma doesn't vanish with time; it lingers in the rhythm of our breath, our bones, our dreams.

This isn't laziness. This is your body remembering—and trying to protect you. The work now is gently teaching it: you are safe now.

High Blood Pressure

This one hits hard in our community. Black Americans are disproportionately affected by hypertension—and it's not just about diet or genetics. It's about stress. Chronic, unrelenting, systemic stress.

You can eat kale and drink water, but if your body is constantly bracing—against racism, classism, generational struggle, microaggressions, and invisible labor—your blood pressure stays high. That's your body saying, "I'm still in danger."

Our ancestors endured unspeakable stress with no release. We carry the residue of that, and now we name it. Not with blame—but with truth and tenderness.

Chronic Pain

Pain that doesn't seem to have a clear cause. Aching joints, tight shoulders, neck stiffness, migraines. It's not all in your head. It's in your body's memory.

Trauma that goes unprocessed often shows up physically. It hides in the muscles, the fascia, the posture. If you've had to hold it together for generations, your body might be holding that tension even now.

Pain can be your body's language—its way of asking you to listen. To slow down. To grieve. To tend.

Anxiety That Seems to Come from Nowhere

That pit in your stomach. That dread that creeps in at the edges of a good day. That racing heart with no clear trigger.

It may not make sense to you, but it makes sense to your nervous system.

Your anxiety might not be about this moment—it might be about a story your body remembers from before you even had language. A warning system passed down like a quilt—stitched with survival, soaked in grief.

But quilts can warm as well as warn. You are allowed to unthread and remove what no longer serves you.

Exhaustion We Can't Explain, Even After Resting

The kind of tired that sleep doesn't fix. The kind of fatigue that feels like it lives in your soul.

This is the exhaustion of generations. The exhaustion of being "strong" when strong just means unsupported. The weariness of vigilance, of spiritual labor, of enduring without pause.

When your ancestors were worked from sunup to sundown, rest became a luxury. When freedom never came with true ease, our people learned to push through pain—to survive, not to thrive.

Now? We're learning to rest. To nap without guilt. To say "I'm tired" and not apologize.

That's not laziness. That's resistance.

Digestive Issues

When you're in survival mode, digestion isn't your body's priority—safety is. Chronic stress disrupts how the gut functions. That can look like constipation, bloating, acid reflux, nausea, or IBS symptoms.

And it's not just biology—it's emotional. The gut is deeply connected to the brain. In many cultures, including ours, we've always said "I feel it in my gut." That's because trauma lives there, too.

What happens when people are malnourished for generations? When food is rationed, withheld, weaponized? When we eat fast, distracted, or only when we feel we've "earned" it? Is chronic obesity in the African American community a surprise?

These patterns don't come from nowhere.

I live with Crohn's disease. As I look back I remember sitting outside the bathroom door, listening helplessly as my grandma cried out in pain while going to the restroom. My cousin and my sister both struggle with gut issues, too. Stomach pain, inflammation, and food that turns against us. And to me, that's no coincidence.

The physical and emotional issues listed above aren't random afflictions. They're echoes resonating from generations forced to live in survival mode. And now, science has a name for it: epigenetic inheritance. Trauma doesn't just shape minds, it can leave marks on our DNA. Through a process called methylation, tiny chemical tags attach to our genes in response to trauma. And those tags? They can be passed down, generation after generation.

So when folks say, "That's just how it is in our family," I say, maybe—but maybe not.

Maybe that's how we had to be.

Maybe that's what trauma wrote into our very cells.

But here's the good news: just as trauma can be passed down, so can healing.

Healing isn't just medical—it's sacred. The nervous system can learn safety. The body can remember joy. And you—you don't have to carry the whole burden alone.

And you know what's wild?

Sometimes we blame ourselves for what we carry.

For not being "strong enough."

For not being "healed yet."

For not praying hard enough. Not being prayerful enough.

But friend—how can you heal from a wound no one ever told you you had?

So let me say this with your whole heart in mind:

You are not broken.
You are not too sensitive.
You are not weak for needing rest or boundaries or space to breathe.

You are walking through a world built on the bones of your ancestors.

A world that told your people they were objects—not souls.

And yet, here you are—feeling, questioning, healing, thriving in your own way.

That matters.

That's revolutionary.

The stories we just heard? They help us understand the patterns we inherited. But they're not the final word. You don't have to keep surviving the way your foremothers did.

You get to heal. You get to choose something new.

But just like trauma, strength can be passed down too. We inherited joy that refused to die. We inherited praise dances in dirt floor churches and lullabies whispered over cotton rows. We inherited the power to keep going—and now we inherit the right to rest.

We'll keep walking this path together—because their journey didn't end with emancipation.

And neither does yours.

CHAPTER 5

From Reconstruction to Modern Day

The Voices at the Table

The wind shifted outside, brushing against the cabin walls like something was coming near.

Mama Feely didn't flinch. She just looked toward the door.

"We gots company," she said softly. "Dey heard we was tellin' de truth. And dey come to have dey say."

One by one, they entered—not as ghosts, but as honored elders. Siney Bonner. Charlie Davis. Wylie Nealy. Robert Falls. Their faces bore the marks of time and struggle, but their presence was steady, their eyes clear. They took their seats around the table, the fire warming their backs, steam rising from fresh cups of mint tea.

I felt something catch in my chest. Gratitude. Grief. Reverence. I looked to Mama Feely, unsure what to say.

"Go on, chile," she said to me. "Ask 'em what they remember. Let 'em tell it in dey own way."

I turned to the first figure, an older woman whose hands were folded calmly in her lap.

"Miss Siney… would you share what freedom was like for you?"

She looked down for a moment, then began.

"Massa John call all de niggers on de plantation 'round him at de big house and he say to 'em, 'Now, you all jes' as free as I is. I ain't your marster no mo'.' Some stayed and some lef'. My daddy stayed wid Marse John till he was called home to glory. Now dey all gone but Siney, and I'se jes' here, waitin' for 'em to call me."

The room fell still.

"She ain't just talkin' about waitin' to die," Mama Feely said, wiping her eye. "She waitin' to be seen. Don't just listen with yo' ears—listen wit yo' heart."

The man seated next to her leaned forward. Charlie Davis. His voice was quiet but resolute.

"When dem Yankees talk bout comin round, my Massa take all we colored boys en all he fast horses en put em back in de woods to de canebrake to hide em from de Yankees... Dey say dey was gwine free de niggers en if it hadn' been for dem, we would been slaves till yet."

"Say your name," Mama Feely said gently.

"Charlie Davis. South Carolina," he replied.

She nodded. "We see you, Charlie."

Then came Wylie Nealy, eyes distant like he was still walking some dusty road.

"I remember so well, how the roads was full of folks walking and walking along when the niggers were freed. Didn't know where they was going. Just going to see about something else somewhere else."

I felt the ache behind his voice—like freedom had come not as a promise, but as a question with no answer.

"Mmm," Mama Feely murmured, shakin' her head slow. "Dat's what happen when dey turn you out wit nothin' but de breath in yo' body. No land, no tools, no place to lay your head. Just sayin' you free, but leavin' you to wander like cattle loosed from a pen, hungry an' hollow."

She looked into the fire, eyes heavy with memory.

"That ain't freedom, baby—dat's a heartbreak dat settle in yo' bones. When you been caged so long, even de open road feel like a trap. Make your spirit stumble, like it forgot how to walk free."

The last to speak was Robert Falls. He straightened in his chair and cleared his throat.

"I begins to think and to know things. And I knowed then I could make a living for my own self, and I never had to be a slave no more."

We all looked at him. Even the fire seemed to lean in.

"Dat right there," Mama Feely said, "is what dey couldn't kill. Dat's de seed. Dat's de Spirit. Dat's hope still speakin' through generations."

I paused and sat with that. Realizing that I am the prayer my ancestors whispered into the night.

I am the song they couldn't sing out loud.

I am the harvest they never lived to see.

And It was enough to change everything.

The room felt full, like memory itself had taken a seat and settled in. We sat in silence for a moment, letting the weight of their stories settle over us like a quilt.

Then Mama Feely stood.

"Thank you," she said, her voice thick with love. "For comin'. For tellin'. For survivin'. We won't forget you."

One by one, our guests rose from the table. Siney, Charlie, Wylie, Robert. They didn't vanish—they passed through, like wind brushing wheat. Their presence lingered, a balm and a charge.

"Dey gone for now," Mama Feely said, pouring the last of the tea, "but dey stories walk with us. And we gon' need dey strength, 'cause the road don't stop here."

She looked at me, then toward the door.

"After slav'ry ended, dey called it Reconstruction—said dey was gon' rebuild de South. But baby, what dey really mean was rebuildin' it for dem. For us? We had to build somethin' outta nothin'. Dey gave us freedom on paper, but tried to snatch it back every time we stood too tall."

She looked off, like she could see it playing out again.

"But we ain't just lay down. No ma'am. We open up schools—real ones. Built churches wit our own hands. Started towns where Black folks could live wit some peace. Some of us even got 'lected to office—senators, congressmen, councilmen. Sat in rooms dey swore we'd never enter. We was dreamin' big, baby. Doin' for ourselves."

She paused, voice lower now.

"But white folks in power couldn't stand to see it. So they brought de hammer down—laws, lynch mobs, and lies. Burned our towns. Stole our land. Called it Redemption, but it was just slav'ry wit a new name. They wanted to tear down everything we was buildin' 'fore it could take root."

Then she fixed her eyes on me, firm and tender.

"So yeah, we made progress—real, holy progress. But we paid fo' every inch wit blood, sweat, and sorrow. Reconstruction weren't jus' a time—it was a battlefield. And we ain't never stopped fightin' really."

I wrapped my hands around the warm mug. The fire had died down, but its heat was still in the room.

"Come on, baby," Mama Feely said gently, pouring the last of the tea. "Let's step into what come next."

We rose from the table and stepped back out into the night. Not because we weren't tired, but because we knew the night wasn't done speaking.

Mama Feely leaned back, her hand resting gently on her chest, eyes closed like she was listening for something. Maybe she was. Maybe it was my turn now.

I wrapped my fingers around my teacup, the warmth grounding me in the night air. "Mama Feely, you had a son, right?" I said, almost in a whisper. "His name was Rufus. Born in 1833, right here in North Carolina. Like you, he was born into slavery."

Mama Feely didn't open her eyes, but I saw her lips curl into a sad sort of smile.

I stared into the last swirls of mint at the bottom of my cup.

"They gave him the surname Norris," I said quietly. "Rufus. Your son."

Mama Feely didn't move, but I could feel her listening.

"And something unusual happened. He was freed in 1856."

I looked at her, trying to meet her gaze, but her eyes remained closed.

"That was five years before the Civil War even started. Why?"

She let out a short, dry laugh and finally cracked an eye open.

"Why you think, baby?" she said, lips curling into something between a smirk and a scowl. "Dey ain't just wake up one day feelin' generous."

I sighed, letting the weight of it sink in.

"I can only guess," I said. "Maybe… maybe because he was blood. Maybe because somebody in that house looked at him and saw themselves."

I paused, knowing that there is a DNA match on Ancestry.com that connects my family to one of Samuel P. Norris's white descendants.

Mama Feely's eyes opened fully now, slow and steady.

"Mmm," she murmured, her voice thick with memory. "They didn't want that kind of truth gettin' out. It'd mean they'd have to see us as kin. Not property. Not labor. But blood."

She looked at me, her gaze steady and sharp.

"And once you see someone as kin, chile... you can't own 'em no mo'."

She paused, her gaze far off. "Dey don't speak on what it really mean... for a woman to carry de child of the man who owned her. Folks don't wanna look dat close. Don't wanna touch de shame of it... or de power, or de lack of it. We ain't have no say. Just prayers whispered through tears and pain we couldn't run from."

She let out a breath and continued.

"But Rufus? He was mine. And dey knew it. Dat's why dey freed him. Maybe it was guilt. Maybe dey was scared what de neighbors would say if'n dey saw dey own blood wearin' chains. But dey ain't never write dat part down."

She looked at me, steady now. "And you know, baby, blood tell de truth even when people won't."

I paused and looked up at the stars, their quiet shimmer no match for the gravity of what had just been shared.

My throat tightened. I turned back to her, eyes stinging.

"Mama Feely…" I whispered, unsure if any words could carry the weight of what I felt. "Thank you."

She tilted her head, waiting.

"Thank you for your courage. For surviving what no one should've had to survive. For loving Rufus, even when everything around you tried to strip you of that right. When he was freed, but you were put in that man's will to be given to his wife when he died. For speaking the truth, when others tried to bury it."

My voice cracked, but I kept going.

"You didn't just birth him—you birthed a line. A whole line that led to me. Without you, I wouldn't be here. And I don't take that lightly. I'm honored—truly honored— to be here with you. To hear you. To carry your story forward."

She didn't say a word right away, but I saw something shift behind her eyes. A softening. Maybe even a release.

It wasn't just history she'd given me—it was herself. Her truth. Her pain. Her power.

And I received it with reverence, holding it like the treasure it was.

The road after emancipation was not paved with justice. My ancestors had to build new lives on the ash-covered soil of slavery, with no restitution, no protection, and no promise of peace. while this is true for the most part, there were exceptions like my 3x great grandfather Rufus, who had land. But I wonder about the protection and peace because that land is no longer in our family.

"Reconstruction," Mama Feely scoffed, shaking her head slowly. "It was a fragile kind of hope. We built schools. Churches. Lil' businesses dat held big dreams. We voted, too. Lord, I remember de first time I cast a ballot… Had to walk past a group of mens dat spit on us and called us nasty names jus' to put my X on dat line. My knees was shakin', but my spine stayed straight. 'Cause it meant somethin'. It meant I meant somethin'."

I nodded, picturing Rufus walking his land with callused hands and quiet dignity.

"We had land," she continued. "Dreamed bold. And we did it all wit de eyes of white resentment burnin' holes through our backs."

I swallowed. "Because they didn't want us to succeed."

"Dey couldn't stand to see it," she said. "So when dem federal troops pulled out in 1877, de devil came struttin' in under a white sheet. Mobs burned our towns. Politicians passed laws to strip us bare. De promise of freedom?" She paused, looking out into the dark. "Swallered up by terror."

I felt a heaviness in my chest. "What must it have been like for them," I whispered, "trying to build dignity and opportunity, while Black codes, lynchings, and Klansmen filled the land like weeds?"

"Chile," Mama Feely said, her voice low, "it was like breathin' with a rope around your neck."

I pictured it: one hand holding a plow, the other holding a newspaper from The Richmond Planet or The Chicago Defender, pages smeared with the blood of another teacher murdered, another church burned, another child orphaned by racial terror.

Then, still… because life demands, still continuing to work.

Mama Feely nodded. "That's how Jim Crow slipped in. Not with chains, but with courtrooms. With lynchin' trees. With back doors marked colored only."

I picked up her rhythm. "Jim Crow didn't need a whip. It had poll taxes. Chain gangs. Laws that turned poverty into prison."

"My great-great-grandmother Molly, and her son Ned, and his wife Maggie—they lived through that," I said. "They raised kids in a world that demanded 'yes ma'am' but gave no dignity back. They labored in fields and factories, forced to smile through the insults just to keep their jobs."

"They couldn't cry at work," Mama Feely murmured.

"Couldn't afford to be angry. Couldn't afford to say no," I echoed.

"So they taught us to be nice," I said. "To work twice as hard. To 'be grateful'—but that gratitude was just grief with a good posture."

Mama Feely opened her eyes again, her voice a low hum from someplace deeper than the ground beneath our feet. "Mmm-hmm. And don't forget, baby—those laws didn't just keep us poor. They kept us afraid. Made our daddies walk small and our mamas teach us to whisper our dreams."

She leaned in, her tone sharp but steady. "Jim Crow wasn't just about what you couldn't do. It was about convincin' you you never could."

I let the truth of her words settle before I spoke again.

"OK," I said slowly. "So when Rufus was freed, he was also given land. And somehow, by the time he died in 1922, he owned 307 acres in Wake County."

Mama Feely raised her eyebrows, a flicker of pride passing across her face.

"That was no small feat," I added. "Not for a man who had once been considered property himself."

I felt the pride. The pain. And still, I pressed on.

"When he passed, his ten children each received land and cash—twenty or thirty acres apiece. But none of that land is in our family today. Not a single acre."

I exhaled slowly, letting the loss hang in the air between us.

"I can only imagine the forces that conspired to take it from us: mismanagement, the Depression, predatory policies, heirs' property, tax sales, discriminatory lending. Jim Crow laws meant to strip away everything we built."

The silence in the night wrapped around us like a thick quilt—old, familiar, and far too heavy to shake off.

I continued, feeling like the griot I was becoming.

"At age thirty, Rufus married Etta, and they had six children. Their daughter, Mary,called Molly, was my great-great-grandmother. Molly had a son named Ned, or Edward. He married Maggie and had four children, including my grandfather, Robert Norris. Maggie died young. Later, Edward had three daughters with another woman. They never married, but I got to know those aunts growing up in Chicago."

I glanced at Mama Feely. "That we ended up in Chicago isn't surprising. Like so many others, our family joined the Great Migration, chasing the promise of better jobs, safer streets, and something like dignity."

Mama Feely opened her eyes, soft and steady. "A lot of us went north," she said. "But the wound came with us."

I nodded. "Yes, ma'am. My grandfather Robert married Melba Walker—despite her people's disapproval. They had four children. The youngest was my mother, Brenda. When Melba died of a heart attack two years after my mom was born, the Walkers took the children. Some say he left heartbroken. Others say he was pushed away. Either way, the family splintered—and the silence that followed spoke volumes."

I took a deep breath. "I didn't know until I was an adult, but after Melba died, my mother and her siblings were placed in foster care. I'm not sure for how long. No one really talks about it. It's not a secret, exactly—but there's a silence there. Like a well-worn mask. Maybe it's pride. Maybe it's pain. Maybe silence was their way of surviving."

The candle between us flickered, and I kept going.

"When my mom was in high school, she met my father, Joe Murdock. His people came up from Mississippi—part of the same migration, with wounds and resilience of their own."

I looked up at Mama Feely. "All these stories. All these people. I wish I had grown up knowing about all this. I wish I had these stories to help me feel rooted and connected to a family arc. Like I belong."

She met my eyes, her voice low and heavy like a hymn sung through grief.

"Dat was de plan all along, baby. To tear us apart—piece by piece. From de land dat held our roots. From each other's arms. From de names of our people an' de stories dat should've been ours to hold. Dey ain't just want to own us... they wanted us forgetful. Like beasts. Wanted us so lost, we couldn't even find ourselves."

She shook her head, slow.

"Dat's what happen when a system don' see you as human. It don' care 'bout your mama's name or your granddaddy's prayers. It just see labor. Just see numbers. And dat kind of erasin'? It don't end with de chains. It keep goin'—through silence, through shame, through de not-knowing."

She placed her hand over her heart.

"But baby, every time you call on your people—by name, by story, even by feelin'—you breakin' dat lie. You rememberin' what dey tried to make us forget."

The truth of it settled deep within me.

"Generational trauma isn't always loud," I said. "Sometimes it shows up in silence at the dinner table. In nervous laughter. In the way we lash out when we speak our truth. It lives in our muscles. In the way we walk into a room, already braced for impact."

I paused, then added, "Our people didn't just survive slavery. They survived Reconstruction, Jim Crow, redlining, poll taxes, and police dogs. My grandparents worked jobs that barely paid and kept smiling through it all. They said 'yes, ma'am' to keep the peace, even while reading headlines about lynchings and arrests. Then they went to work for folks who'd fire them for less than a frown."

I looked at her, my voice soft.

"You know, Mama Feely… my parents were just kids during the Civil Rights Movement. They saw all of it—on those old black-and-white TVs. The marches. The speeches. Bloody bodies on the Edmund Pettus Bridge. They watched kids, not much older than them, get blasted with fire hoses, arrested, spit on."

I paused, shaking my head.

"And still… come Monday morning, they were expected to show up at school like everything was fine. Sit on city buses driven by men who told them to move to the back. Smile at teachers who wouldn't even call on them. They learned fast—who you were at home couldn't always be who you were in public."

I looked down at my hands, then back up at her.

"That kind of split? It doesn't just go away. I think we've been carrying it ever since."

"Code-switching wasn't a trend," I said. "It was survival."

Mama Feely nodded slow, like she was agreeing with something her spirit already knew.

"Mmm-hmm. You right, baby. That split run deep. Been teachin' us for generations how to wear masks just to make it through. Smile when we wanna scream. Shrink ourselves so we don't seem like a threat. That ain't weakness—that's survival."

She reached across the table, her hand warm and steady on mine.

"But you ain't gotta keep carryin' all dat. Not by yo'self. What dey passed down in silence, you get to name out loud. An' every time you speak it, every time you tell de truth of what dey lived through—you stitchin' dem pieces back together."

She smiled then, soft but sure.

"Dat's how we heal, baby. One memory at a time."

And now? I see how I still carry it—that deep need to be agreeable, that ache to be accepted. I think about how many times I've smiled when I really wanted to scream. How often I've pushed myself to the edge, trying to prove I belonged. How I've stayed quiet—not because I didn't have something to say, but because I didn't want to be seen as angry.

That's survival—passed down, practiced, perfected.

But here's the thing: when those survival responses become our norm—when hypervigilance, people-pleasing, and emotional numbness feel like personality traits—we don't always recognize them for what they are. But they are the residue of something older. Not the kind of trauma that explodes, but the kind that drips slow... steady... quiet. The kind that therapists call Complex PTSD. The kind that doesn't come from one moment—but from a lifetime of being told to shrink, and systems set up to reinforce that command.

I leaned in, my voice low.

"But survival... that's not the same as living."

Mama Feely nodded.

"No, baby. It ain't."

She paused,

"Back then, we didn't call it no code-switchin'. We just called it doin' what you had to do to make it home alive."

We've inherited that shape-shifting. And that inheritance didn't begin with us—it was passed down through systems that punished our resistance and demanded our performance. The body remembers what the mind tries to forget. That bone-deep awareness. The nervous system trained not to make waves.

Beloved, you are not "selling out.". You are not "too sensitive."

You are living the echo of generations who had to hide their brilliance, swallow their rage, and pretend not to notice when dignity was denied.

They say this is a post-racial society. We had a Black president. There are Black CEOs and magazine covers full of melanin and money. But the residue of dehumanization doesn't disappear with symbolism.

When a girl gets suspended for wearing braids or when someone says "I don't see color" like it's a virtue…

That's not progress. That's a system still trying to control not just our behavior—but our bodies.

As Daniel Hill points out in White Awake, colorblindness doesn't erase racism—it erases people. It minimizes the unique racial and cultural heritage of individuals and promotes a so-called "neutral" approach that ignores the realities of lived experience and generational struggle. And the truth is, you can't fix what you refuse to see.

I remember watching the protests unfold in 2020. One moment in particular stays with me: a young Black woman stood in front of burning buildings, sirens blaring behind her, tears streaming down her face. Her voice shook as she said, "They need to be glad that we just want equality—and not revenge."

That hit me hard. Because beneath the pain, what she said was voiced a longing to matter. A longing to be seen as a human who matters.

From Reconstruction to redlining… from Jim Crow to mass incarceration… from lynchings to microaggressions, we have always had to fight to be seen as fully human. Not a threat. Not a problem to solve. Not a checkbox. Just people, deserving of dignity.

And we've used everything available to us in that fight.

We've resisted through music, protest, food, education, sisterhood, and the church. We've held onto each other when systems tried to tear us apart. Through it all, family—chosen and blood—has been the thread that kept us going.

Even now, that fight continues. We're still fighting for safe schools, for housing we can keep, for mental health care that sees us, for the right to breathe without justification—for rest, for peace, for the freedom just to exist.

But this isn't only about struggle. It's also about how we've learned to strategize, to love, and to stay rooted. Our anger is justified, but our joy matters, too. Our rest is essential. Our healing is sacred.

Resilience isn't just surviving the storm. It's learning how to keep going, how to hold joy in the midst of grief, how to build something new out of what tried to break us.

Mama Feely looked at me then, her eyes full of fire and tenderness.

"You cain't outrun what you ain't faced," she said. "But if you look it in the eye, you just might find your power."

And that's what brings us to this point in the journey. We've named the wounds. We've seen the patterns in our bodies, our families, our silence, and our striving.

Then the question becomes: What now?

Outside, the wind stirred the trees. Inside, the weight of it all wrapped around us.

"We've fought so long just to be seen," I whispered. "From Reconstruction to hashtags. From school suspensions over hair extensions, to police bullets, to protest chants. And still, we're told to keep our heads down, to move on, to forget the past."

"But I remember," I said, my voice steady. "I remember Rufus. I remember the land. And maybe that's enough for now."

Mama Feely reached for my hand and held it.

"Tomorrow," she said, "we rise."

And in that quiet moment, with the fire dying and our souls heavy with history, I believed her.

As the flames gave way to glowing embers and her hand slipped from mine, I sat in the stillness a while longer, heart full and eyes wet.

And now, beloved sister, I turn to you.

You've been sitting at this table with us all along—listening, feeling, remembering things you didn't know you knew. You may not have the name "Rufus" in your family tree. You may not know the stories of land lost or kin scattered. But I know you've felt the weight of what's been passed down. You carry it in your body. In your breath. In the way you brace yourself before walking into a room that wasn't built for you.

This story isn't just mine.

It's yours too.

You've felt the lump in your throat when the silence was too familiar. You've held your breath just to get through the day.

So let me say this plainly:

You are not broken.

You are not imagining things.

What you're carrying has a history.

And you're allowed to lay it down.

Let's name it.

Let's understand it.

Let's begin to heal—together.

Acknowledgment

The voices you've heard at Mama Feely's table in these chapters are not inventions of my pen. They belong to our ancestors. In the 1930s, the Federal Writers' Project of the Works Progress Administration sent interviewers into towns and backroads to gather the stories of those who had lived through slavery. Their words — trembling, weary, resilient, sometimes sharp with pain, sometimes warm with memory — were written down and preserved.

It is from those Slave Narratives that I have drawn the voices you encountered here. I set them at the table with Mama Feely as they were recorded by the WPA, not to dramatize them, but to honor them. To remind us that our healing journey is tied to their witness. These were real people, with real names, who gave us their truth. Their testimonies live on in the public record through the Library of Congress and the National Humanities Center.

When we listen to them, we remember that the story of survival has never been ours alone. It has always been a chorus.

Selah

(A pause, a breath, a turning inward)

You've inherited the weight of history.

Now come, Sis. Let's begin to lay it down.

Part 2 : Awakening

CHAPTER 6

Awakening

I didn't get a formal goodbye from Mama Feely. She didn't need one.

After all the stories were told, after the fire in her cabin softened to glowing coals, I turned to her. My arms wrapped around her solid frame. She was strong and steady like the roots of a very old tree. She smelled like woodsmoke and peppermint. Her arms didn't tremble when they held me. She just rocked me for a moment, like she had done it before—for her children, her kin, maybe even for someone like me in a dream she never wrote down.

We didn't say much. But something passed between us in that embrace. Something eternal and quiet and powerful. Something like peace.

When I woke up the next morning, I went into the bathroom, rubbed the sleep from my eyes, and stared into the mirror. At first, it was just me—swollen lids, dry lips, curls doing their own thing. But then I looked closer. And I saw her. I saw Mama Feely in my face. Not just in the shape of my nose or the curve of my brow, but in my eyes. There was a knowing there that hadn't been there before. A quiet strength I hadn't noticed until now.

The reckoning had done its work.

It hadn't just taught me history. It had handed me a mirror. And I couldn't look away.

There comes a point when the learning starts to settle into your bones. When the grief softens into a steady hum. When you stop asking, "What happened to us?" and start asking, "What does this mean for me now?"

That's where I found myself, at a threshold. I share this not because my experience is everyone's, but because I know I'm not alone. If any of this feels familiar to you, know that your awakening is valid, even if it looks different from mine.

This chapter marks that threshold. If you've made it this far, you've already done something sacred. You've remembered. You've mourned. You've peeled back the layers of silence and witnessed truths that were never meant to be hidden. And maybe, like me, you're tired. Maybe your chest is tight from the weight of it all.

If you need to stop here, I understand. You've already done the holy work of acknowledging the wound.

But if something in you is still stirring, if there's a whisper saying, there's more then I want to invite you to come a little further.

You see, I'm not called to dismantle every broken system. That work is noble. And it's heavy. It takes a long time, and a lot of people, and a stomach for the long game. There are gifted folks who carry that mantle, who hold protest signs and policy papers in each hand.

That's not my lane.

My lane is for those who are trying to figure out how to live. How to breathe and thrive and love in the world as it is, without giving up hope for what it could become. My work is about equipping people to reclaim themselves, to use the tools they already have, and to build something beautiful right in the middle of the mess.

The truth is, we may not be able to prove a straight line between what happened centuries ago and what's happening inside us now—but it would be foolish not to look. We don't need perfect causation to honor the deep connections between our history and our present.

Correlation doesn't explain everything, but silence explains nothing.

So this is where we begin again.

Not just with knowledge, but with power.

Not just with remembering, but with awakening.

What Was Lost or Adapted Due to Slavery

To fully understand who we are today, we must acknowledge what was stolen, silenced, or reshaped in the crucible of slavery. We were not born broken. Our ancestors did not come from nothing. West African societies had systems—languages, medicine, spiritual practices, agricultural knowledge, artistry, music. They didn't just believe in God, they walked with the ancestors, they danced their prayers, they raised children in community, and they tended to life with wisdom passed down through generations.

But that richness, the very essence of who we were, was deemed dangerous or inferior by colonizers. Through forced migration, violent assimilation, and cultural erasure, much of what made us whole was fractured or reframed to serve systems that needed us to forget our power.

Take midwifery, for example. Midwives were once honored women. They were keepers of life, tradition, and sacred knowledge. They knew how to position babies, when to pray, and which herbs to use. Their work wasn't just physical, it was spiritual. But during and after slavery, their wisdom was cast as backwards, unscientific, even "voodoo." Hospitals and Western medicine became the new authority, and Black midwives were pushed to the margins or disappeared altogether. We didn't just lose a birthing tradition—we lost a spiritual connection to creation itself.

This loss was not just about birth practices. It was about survival. Without trusted advocates at their side, Black women entered a system that often dismissed their pain and ignored their voices. The results were deadly then, and they remain deadly now. Black mothers are still more likely to die from pregnancy-related complications, and Black infants are still more likely to die in their first year of life. These are not accidents of biology. They are the enduring legacy of a system that chose control over care, erasure over tradition.

When we lost midwifery as the center of Black birthing, we didn't just lose a practice, we lost a lifeline. We lost the protection of women who understood the body and the spirit together. We lost a layer of safety, a shield against neglect. We lost a spiritual connection to creation itself, a way of honoring life that saw Black mothers and babies as worthy of sacred care.

Our healing practices—the salves, teas, and rituals that soothed generations—were once central to community care. What was ours was plant medicine and energy work. What we heard instead was that we were primitive. Superstitious. Even evil. Hoodoo and rootwork, born of survival and divine knowledge, were criminalized or mocked. Today, essential oils and herbalism are everywhere—but we'll talk more about how they came back in the next chapter.

Then there was our language. We created African American Vernacular English (AAVE) not out of ignorance, but brilliance—blending African linguistic structures with English in ways that conveyed nuance, culture, and emotion. But in classrooms and courtrooms, AAVE was called "improper." We were told to speak "correctly," and we learned to code-switch if we wanted to be seen as smart or worthy. The linguistic genius of our people was stripped of its dignity, its spiritual rhythm flattened into grammar lessons.

I felt this tension early on. When my family moved back to inner-city Chicago after my dad left the Air Force, I was seven years old. Having grown up in mostly white spaces, I had never been in a majority-Black environment before, nor had I been exposed to AAVE the way my new peers had. I remember being ostracized by would-be playmates. I was smug about my "proper" English, thinking it made me better somehow. The sad part is that I didn't realize until much later that what I dismissed as "broken" was actually a legacy of West African language structures, a cultural inheritance woven into our very speech. My pride in "correctness" was really evidence of how deeply white supremacy had shaped me, blinding me to the beauty and brilliance of my own people's tongue.

And music, the one thing we were rarely completely forbidden to have, still wasn't left untouched. Our spirituals, ring shouts, and polyrhythms held our prayers, our pain, and our coded resistance. But even then, enslavers tried to censor our songs or co-opt them for control. Later, Black gospel was deemed too emotional, blues too sinful, jazz too wild. Yet it was our rhythm that shaped global music, our harmonies that birthed entire genres.

Even our bodies were not safe from redefinition. What was ours—our curves, coils, skin—was labeled ugly, unprofessional, excessive. Our hair was "unruly," our features mocked in minstrel shows and racist cartoons that me and my GenX compatriots laughed at but did not understand. The same hips they used to breed us were the ones they later deemed vulgar. We were told to cover up, to straighten out, to shrink ourselves.

We also lost names—not just the names of ancestors, but the act of naming as a sacred ritual. In the ledgers of slaveholders, our people were listed by gender, age, and market value. "Male, 10, worth $300." No name. No story. No mother's whisper over a newborn's head. That's why memorials like the Equal Justice Initiative's National Memorial for Peace and Justice, with their lists of names, are so powerful. Names insist that lives were lived, that someone laughed, struggled, danced, and dreamed. Children. Elders. Dreamers. Storytellers.

These aren't just historical facts, they are spiritual wounds. Wounds that still inform how we see ourselves and how the world sees us. We inherited not only the trauma, but also the disconnection. And yet, not all was lost.

There is reclamation in the way a grandmother hums while stirring a pot…

In the way we rock babies rhythmically on our hips…

In the way we gather around death with food and song and testimony…

…and we hear the echo of home.

The Fallout From Not Knowing Who We Are as a People

There is a cost to not knowing who you are.

Not just in the broad strokes of culture or history, but in the quiet corners of your own heart. In how you handle conflict. In how you see yourself in the mirror. In how you move through the world, apologizing for taking up space or trying so hard to prove your worth that you burn yourself out before noon.

When you've been disconnected from your story, when no one taught you the names of your people, or gave you the language to hold your pain, you improvise. You build your identity from what's around you. Whether that be from media stereotypes, classroom labels, or workplace code-switching. You survive. But often at the cost of clarity, confidence, and peace.

That disconnection doesn't just linger in the background—it spills over into every part of life. You see it in how so many of us become emotional reservoirs for others, never having been taught to care for our own feelings. You see it at the dinner table, where silence wraps itself around unspeakable things, and everyone pretends not to notice the weight that hovers in the room. It surfaces in the fierce independence that tells the world, "I don't need anybody," even while we quietly break under the pressure. It takes the shape of loudness misread as confidence, or quiet mistaken for humility, when really, both are just trauma in disguise.

This disconnection shows up in the way our children are over-disciplined at school, in how the criminal justice system swallows our loved ones, and in the ways Black girls are told their voices are too sharp, that they are too fast, too much—for daring to speak truth too early.

When you don't know who you are, the world is eager to define you. And more often than not, it does so by what you lack—by your struggle, your behaviors, your appearance, or your pain. Labels like "too sensitive," "too angry," "too much," or "unmotivated" are thrown around carelessly, when what they're really describing is a sacred self struggling to break through, burdened by a weight it was never meant to carry.

And that weight? We didn't choose it. But we inherited it.

We inherited the pressure to overachieve, to outperform, to be twice as good for half as much. We inherited strategies that once kept our ancestors alive in the face of danger. Strategies that, in moments of safety or vulnerability, now hold us hostage. Hypervigilance made sense when the threat was real and constant. Silence was once a shield when speaking out could cost your life. Self-denial was the price of being allowed to remain.

But today, those same traits are praised in certain settings and pathologized in others. We are urged to "heal," often without any acknowledgment of the logical origins of our wounds.

So let me tell you the truth: You are not broken. You are responding to centuries of disruption. You are not at fault for what you inherited. But you do carry the sacred responsibility of deciding what you will pass on.

This is the work now. Not just surviving, not just understanding, but choosing. Choosing to pause, to examine what you've been handed, to hold it up to the light, and to release what no longer serves you.

Because when you know who you are, the performance can stop. You begin to heal, to honor, to integrate. You shift from fragmentation to wholeness.

This is the fallout of disconnection. But it is also the threshold of reclamation.

And it begins by remembering: you come from more than pain. You come from people who endured the unthinkable and still preserved their dignity. You come from love passed down in lullabies and rhythm embedded in your walk. You come from brilliance, long buried but still burning.

And that brilliance? It's still yours.

Before we can reclaim what was lost, we have to be willing to look, gently and curiously into the fog of what remains. That's where history becomes personal.

Getting Acquainted With Your People and History

It's hard to know where you're going if you've never been told where you come from.

For many of us, history doesn't feel like an heirloom. It feels like a blur. Names missing. Stories distorted. Faces lost in the margins of slave registers and census forms. It can feel like trying to piece together a puzzle when half the box was burned generations ago.

And yet—there's power in looking.

Even if you don't have a full family tree or a list of ancestors going back generations, you can begin with the soil under your feet. With the rhythms in your body. With the traditions that show up in your kitchen, your speech, your church, your laughter, your grief. The stories might have been fragmented, but they weren't destroyed.

The Loss of Names and the Power of Remembering

During slavery, Black people were stripped of their names. Men, women, and children were listed in inventories as "Negro female, age 7, $400" or "Negro male, age 19, $1700." Lives reduced to numbers. Love, dreams, and personalities flattened into property. Many enslaved people were not even allowed to name their children, or their names were forcibly changed to reflect the name of their "owner."

That's why the first time I saw Feely's name in the family history documents I was blessed to receive, it hit me like a thunderclap. I had read those painful descriptions of enslaved people reduced to age and dollar signs—souls flattened into property lines. And then, suddenly, there was Feely. A name. An identity. A woman who lived, who endured, who passed something of herself down to me. In that moment, the silence of erasure broke open, and I felt the holy weight of connection: You come from me. You are not forgotten.

Names matter. They say, I was here. They carry dignity. They restore personhood. Seeing Feely's name written down was like being handed a fragment of the past that had survived fire and flood. It was more than genealogy; it was healing.

That's why, in our own journeys, even learning the name of one ancestor, one birthplace, one migration story—can feel like holding a sacred relic. You don't need the whole record to begin. You need a willingness to look.

The Reclamation Begins Where You Are

Start with what you know. Ask your elders. Pull out the family photo albums. Search the Freedmen's Bureau records, the 1870 Census, DNA tests if you're open to them. But beyond the documents, also ask:

- What foods did your grandmother cook?
- What stories about Uncle Charles were told over and over but never fully explained?
- What songs got sung while cleaning, rocking, weeping?

These are records, too.

And even if you can't trace your lineage directly, you can still claim your inheritance. Not just of pain—but of wisdom. Of creativity. Of fierce love and sacred resistance.

You can still say: I come from somewhere. I come from somebody.

And if you can't reach back or talk to any elders, remember—y'all are my play cousins. You can share my lineage.

Ubuntu and the Soul of African Identity

John Mbiti, a Kenyan theologian and philosopher, once wrote, "I am because we are, and because we are, therefore I am." That's the heart of Ubuntu—a philosophy that says identity is never formed in isolation. We exist in relationship. We are shaped by community, by memory, by shared responsibility.

This is a different framework than what we're often taught in the West. Individualism tells us to "pull ourselves up by the bootstraps." But Ubuntu says, There's no such thing as boots without a people to walk with.

In many West African traditions, children aren't just raised by their parents, they're raised by the village. Elders are not discarded; they are consulted. Grief is not silent; it is shared. Naming ceremonies, coming-of-age rituals, communal lament—all of these are ways of saying: You belong. You are known.

We may have lost some of those traditions—but the echo remains.

You hear it in the call and response of a Black church service.

You feel it when your auntie corrects you with love in her eyes.

You see it at a funeral repast.

You carry it when you call out your cousin while playing spades at the cookout.

A Note on Shame, Silence, and Starting Over

Some of us carry shame because we don't know our history. We feel disconnected, embarrassed, even disqualified. We think: Who am I to reclaim a heritage I can't even trace?

Let that go.

You are not the one who cut the cord.

You are the one brave enough to go looking for it.

And if the trauma in your family line has made you afraid to dig, that's okay too. Go slow. Be gentle. Healing is not a sprint. You can begin with the parts that feel safe and expand from there.

Remember: even if you don't know the names of your ancestors, they know yours.

Mapping the Journey: Racial Identity Development

Awakening doesn't happen all at once. For many of us, it unfolds in stages—slowly, painfully, beautifully—as we untangle who we are from what we were taught to believe about ourselves.

Psychologists Derald Wing Sue and David Sue offer a helpful guide for this process. Their Racial/Cultural Identity Development Model describes the emotional and cognitive stages that people of color often pass through on the journey toward a secure and healthy racial identity. You may see yourself in one of these stages. Or, like me, you may recognize that you've moved in and out of them over time.

Conformity is where many of us begin—not because we lack pride, but because we were taught to survive. In this stage, we internalize the values of the dominant culture. We learn to straighten our hair, avoid "talking Black," and downplay our heritage. We might even feel ashamed of it. For years, I thought success meant assimilation. I didn't hate my skin, but I hated my hair. I spent time and money torturing it into something it was never meant to be—chasing a look I had naturally, just in a different form.

But life, as it often does, pushes us into **Dissonance**. Something doesn't add up. Maybe it's the moment we're followed in a store. Maybe it's the sting of a teacher's assumptions, or a cop's glare, or the growing discomfort of watching a colleague say something reckless while we smile and swallow our truth. We begin to question the rules we've been playing by. We ask: Is it really me who's wrong, or is the system broken?

Then comes **Resistance and Immersion**—a fire stage. We reject what no longer fits. We search for truth in Black literature, Black theology, Black art, Black ancestors. We stop trying to blend in and start standing out. We might become angry. We might withdraw from white spaces or question every institution we once

120

trusted. For some, it feels like a cultural baptism. For others, it's a lonely wilderness.

Eventually, we reach **Introspection**. The pendulum swings inward. We begin to ask, How do I honor my heritage while still being fully myself? We start integrating—not erasing complexity, but learning to hold it. We may still critique oppressive systems, but we also soften toward others on their journey, even if they're behind us or ahead of us.

Finally, there is **Integrative Awareness**. In this stage, there is rootedness. We no longer perform our identity. We embody it. We navigate the world with both clarity and compassion. We know who we are. We don't need permission. We're not trying to "pass" or prove. We've reclaimed what was stolen and made peace with what can't be recovered.

These stages aren't linear. You might move forward, then back. You might revisit an earlier stage when faced with new pain or insight. That's okay. Growth is not a straight line—it's a spiral. It deepens.

So wherever you are, you're not late. You're not wrong. You're on a sacred journey of remembering who you've always been.

From Awareness to Empowerment

There comes a moment when knowledge softens into wisdom—when what you've learned starts to live in your body, not just in your mind. This chapter has been about that moment. The sacred shift from understanding to becoming.

Because once you've looked back—once you've faced the weight of what was taken, what was hidden, what was lost—it becomes impossible to go back to sleep. You begin to see the world differently. You begin to see yourself differently.

You've traced the outline of your story across time and memory. You've seen how names were stolen, how traditions were demonized, how pain got passed down like a family recipe no one likes but everyone kept repeating. You've seen how silence isn't neutral. How forgetting costs something. How the past echoes even when it hasn't been named out loud.

And yet—here you are. Still breathing. Still becoming.

There's no neat resolution here. Awakening doesn't come with a bow on top. It comes with choice. With clarity. With the quiet realization that you no longer have to perform for a place at the table. You can build your own.

You don't need to know every name in your lineage to stand in the truth that you are descended from survivors, visionaries, healers, and keepers of memory. You don't need a fully mapped family tree to know that you were never meant to live rootless. The fact that you are here, asking deeper questions, is proof enough that your spirit remembers.

You've witnessed the harm. But you are not only what happened to you.

You are also what's rising in you now.

This isn't about fixing yourself. It's about finally seeing yourself—clearly, wholly, without shame.

It's about asking: Now that I know where I come from, who do I want to become?

That's the invitation. Not to do it perfectly. Not to undo centuries of damage in a day. But to make one honest choice at a time. To name what no longer serves you. To reclaim what was hidden. To lay down what was never yours to carry.

You are not broken. You are responding.

You are not behind. You are awakening.

You are not lost. You are returning—to your people, to your truth, to your own voice.

And if you need to rest here for a while, that's perfectly fine. But when you're ready, we'll keep going. Because there's more to explore. There's more to unlearn. There's more to remember.

In the next chapter, we'll begin to question the cultural waters we were told were the standard. Because before you can fully reclaim yourself, you must know what you've been shaped by. You must be willing to name what you're no longer willing to center.

We've walked the path. We've reckoned with the past.

Now we begin again—with eyes open, shoulders back, and roots intact.

You're not just waking up. You're coming home.

CHAPTER 7

Decentering Whiteness

Naming the Tension

I've wrestled with whether or not to write this chapter. Not because I doubt its truth, but because saying it aloud feels dangerous. Risky in a way that only a Black woman who has spent her life surviving white-dominant spaces can understand. There is a cost to truth-telling when the room was never designed for you to speak freely.

For most of my life, I knew how to be considered "safe." Not too loud. Not angry. Not intimidating. Smart, articulate, agreeable. The kind of Black woman described, though never directly, as "one of the good ones." No one had to say the words. I could feel the relief ripple through the air whenever I smiled instead of frowned, soothed instead of challenged, stayed composed instead of letting my anger show. I could feel it in the way eyes relaxed when I adjusted myself to fit the mold, when I wore clothes that didn't draw attention, when I handled conflict without showing the storm inside me. There was an invisible system of rewards and punishments that trained me to believe belonging meant swallowing rage and carrying other people's comfort.

The truth is, that supposed safety was never free. It came at a cost. A cost to my authenticity. My voice. My right to exist without apology or explanation. Every time I shrank myself to keep the peace, I paid in pieces of myself.

That is why this chapter matters. Because I know I'm not alone. I know you've felt it too, The pressure to dim your light so others won't flinch, to bend yourself into shapes that never belonged to you, to thrive in a system that was never built for your flourishing. Many of us have survived by making ourselves palatable, and many of us are bone-tired from the labor of it.

This chapter is not an educational resource for white readers. It is an offering to us, for us. A place to name aloud what so many of us have carried quietly. To whisper, shout, and testify the truth: there is nothing wrong with you. The fault does not live in your skin, your hair, your laughter, or your way of being. The culture around you was not created to celebrate you. Their standards are not your standards. Their values are not your values.

In the pages ahead, we will name the water we've been swimming in. Not to blame ourselves for being wet, but to finally dry off. To reclaim what whiteness tried to erase. To remember that our worth, our rhythm, our beauty, and our brilliance were never dependent on fitting into a mold that was never ours in the first place.

The Old Fish and the Water

There's a parable I've come to love. It is simple in words but profound in what it reveals. Two young fish are swimming along when they pass an older fish who nods at them and says, "Morning, boys. How's the water?" The two younger fish keep swimming, and then one turns to the other and asks, "What's water?"

The brilliance of this parable is that it captures what so many of us experience as Black people in America. We are immersed in something so total, so constant, so all-encompassing that we do not always know how to name it. It surrounds us, presses against us, and shapes our lives in ways so subtle and so constant that it can feel invisible. Unless someone points to it directly, we may not even recognize it is there.

When I first encountered this story, I felt something in my chest loosen. Finally, I had language for an experience I had lived but could not fully explain. The parable named the water for me. It named the unseen but ever-present culture we have been submerged in from the very beginning. It described the way whiteness functions in our society—not always as an individual act, but as an environment, an atmosphere, a current that moves around us and within us.

This chapter is about learning to see that water. And not just any water, but the cultural water that defines what is considered normal, respectable, intelligent, beautiful, or even godly. We are told that these values are universal. We are taught to believe that the dominant ways of working, speaking, worshiping, or relating are simply the way things should be. But when we look closely, when we slow down enough to question, we begin to realize that those so-called universal standards are not neutral at all. They are cultural. And they are rooted in whiteness.

By whiteness, I am not referring to individual white people or the shade of skin they carry. I am speaking of a framework, a cultural design. Whiteness is the system that elevates certain values as superior, while quietly labeling others as inferior or inappropriate. It is what some describe as white dominant culture or white supremacy culture. These assumptions have been normalized to such a degree that even those who suffer under them—Black folks, Indigenous folks, people of color—often absorb them without realizing it. We breathe them in as if they are oxygen. We accept them as gospel truth without ever pausing to ask, "Whose gospel is this, and who does it serve?"

When I finally began to see the water, something broke open inside me. I realized that the rules I had been taught to live by—the ones that told me to be polished but never passionate, disciplined but never too spiritual, smart but never too outspoken—were not created with me in mind. They were created to sustain a system that was never interested in my thriving. That realization felt like freedom. I did not have to apologize for being too expressive, too communal, too spiritual, too Black. I could stop believing the lie that there was something wrong with me.

Seeing the water gave me a new way to understand myself. I began to see that I was not a misfit or a mistake. I was someone living in a foreign land, fluent in its language but never truly at home in its values. That recognition did not remove the harshness of the world around me, but it did give me the gift of self-compassion. It reminded me that I am not broken. I am not deficient. I am not "too much" or "not enough." I am simply not white. And that, in itself, is not a flaw. It is by God's own design.

What Is White Culture and Why Must We Decenter It?

Once you begin to see the water, you cannot unsee it. The air feels heavier, the expectations begin to show their cracks, and the norms you once accepted without question suddenly look strange. What once seemed natural begins to look absurd. You start to ask questions you never thought to ask: Why is professionalism measured by the sound of my voice instead of the depth of my character? Why is timeliness valued more than truth? Why is vulnerability treated as weakness and silence as strength? Why are we told that the King's English is divine, while the rhythm of our own tongues is dismissed as broken?

What becomes clear is this: what we call "normal" is not neutral. It is cultural. And in America, that culture is rooted in whiteness. To decenter whiteness is to stop treating it as the default measure of goodness, truth, beauty, or professionalism. Decentering whiteness widens the table. It doesn't flip the hierarchy, it removes the hierarchy altogether.

Professionalism, common sense, high standards, objectivity—these are not universal truths. They are white cultural norms dressed up as absolutes, taught to us as the only right way to live and work. They dominate our schools, workplaces, churches, therapy rooms, and even our imaginations. They are so deeply woven into the fabric of American institutions that we forget to ask where they came from or who benefits from them.

The National Museum of African American History and Culture once tried to name these cultural assumptions out loud. They published an infographic titled Aspects

128

and Assumptions of Whiteness in the United States. It listed traits such as rugged individualism, the nuclear family, the Protestant work ethic, an obsession with objectivity, linear time, conflict avoidance, competition, and perfectionism. The intention was to spark reflection. It was a tool to help people see the water. But the backlash was immediate and fierce. Conservative media personalities accused the museum of being racist. One person called the chart "absolutely insane." The pressure mounted until the museum pulled it and issued a statement of clarification.

That moment revealed something essential: whiteness does not like to be seen. Its power lies in invisibility. It insists on being the standard, not one culture among many, but the culture that defines the rest. And when you name it, when you shine a light on its mechanisms, it squirms under the glare and resists accountability.

This is what makes decentering white culture both difficult and necessary. To decenter whiteness is to declare that its values are not divine or objective, but human inventions, designed to uphold certain systems of power. It is to acknowledge that this cultural framework was never neutral. It was never created with all of us in mind.

And what happens when you live in a culture that constantly evaluates you through a lens that was never meant for your flourishing? If your values are rooted in communal care, in expressive spirituality, in storytelling as truth, or in intuitive wisdom, you are often told you are too much, too emotional, too informal, too soft, too undisciplined. The very ways you embody life and spirit are measured as deficiencies because they do not align with the dominant template.

Here is the truth whiteness works to keep hidden: Black culture is not lesser. It is simply different. It is relational, embodied, rhythmic, intuitive, ancestral, communal, and spiritual. These qualities are strengths, not flaws. Yet for centuries, we have been told to suppress them. We have been taught to code-switch, to shrink, to translate ourselves in order to survive.

The cost of this adaptation is profound. Assimilation into a culture that once debated whether we were human will never bring wholeness. You cannot heal in soil that was cultivated to deny your humanity. You cannot find peace by molding yourself into values that were built to erase you. Healing does not grow in that ground.

Our healing grows in different soil—the soil of our ancestors, where music was prayer, where stories carried truth, where community held each other, where God was found not in erasure but in expression. To decenter whiteness is to choose that ground. It is to choose life-giving soil over barren earth. It is the beginning of remembering ourselves as whole, as worthy, as sacred, and as enough.

The Psychic Toll of Belonging Nowhere

To be Black in America is to live in a body that remembers. Even when we press forward, even when we put on our best face, even when we convince ourselves that everything is fine, the body keeps its own record. Our nervous systems carry the weight of what has been done to us. Our muscles, our sleep, our sense of safety—all of them echo the memory of a history that was never healed.

Sometimes the world calls it anxiety. Sometimes it is labeled hypervigilance, depression, or burnout. But often it is ancestral memory. It is the vigilance passed down from generations who knew what it meant to be punished for existing. It is the tightening in the chest that comes from knowing what can happen when you are perceived as a threat, not because of your actions, but simply because of your skin. It is the hyper-awareness that develops after centuries of being watched, judged, punished, and silenced. We inherit those survival strategies in our very bones.

I once read a meme that said: "Being Black in America is like being in an abusive relationship with a country." I felt that truth deeply. To love a nation that does not always love us back is its own kind of trauma. It is not just historical—it is present tense. It is daily. It is alive right now.

We are asked to pledge allegiance to systems that never pledged themselves to our ancestors. We are asked to celebrate the very places where our people were enslaved, segregated, and violated. We are told to "just move on" while the wounds we are asked to forget continue shaping our schools, our neighborhoods, our healthcare, our jobs, and our churches. We are expected to be grateful in the face of structures that still deny our dignity. What does that do to a soul?

It fragments. It tears at the core of who we are. It leaves us caught between pretending everything is fine and carrying the truth like a hidden weight. It trains us to smile when we want to scream, to work twice as hard for half the credit, to sit politely in rooms that have no intention of honoring us, to extend peace when all we have been handed is pressure. This constant performance becomes second nature. But beneath it lives a silent question: Am I too angry? Too Black? Too much?

The real question is not what is wrong with us. The real question is: what does it cost to live in a culture that was never designed to celebrate our existence? That cost shows up in our health, in our relationships, in our very breath. It is a psychic toll that robs joy and sows doubt. And yet, even under that weight, we have created beauty. We have raised families, built communities, birthed music, carried faith, and told stories that refused to be silenced. We have survived, and in surviving we have crafted meaning.

But survival alone is not the end of the story. If you are reading these words and feeling weary, I want you to know that you are not imagining it. You are not too sensitive. You are not broken. You are awakening. What feels like sorrow rising is the truth surfacing. And there is no healing without truth. There is no liberation without lament.

The good news is this: once you realize the trauma is not coming from you, you can stop blaming yourself. You can lay down the shame of thinking you are defective. You can begin to reclaim who you were before distortion, before this water tried to tell you that you were never meant to swim. You can begin the long journey back to yourself.

I carried this trauma for much of my life without having words for it. It showed up as silence. It showed up as perfectionism. It showed up as the frantic need to fix everything before it fell apart. I thought it was just my personality, just my flaw. But then, in one moment of raw honesty, it rose to the surface. My body spoke before my mouth could. The water became visible, and I realized how close I was to drowning. That moment changed everything.

The Pit Vipers in the Room

My deepest reckoning did not come from a book, a sermon, or a protest march. It came during a graduate counseling course, in the middle of an exercise that was supposed to be routine. Our assignment was to participate in live group therapy— each of us both client and observer. The purpose was to practice presence, listening, and reflection. I thought I knew what to expect. I did not.

We were still a new group, finding our rhythm, sharing cautiously but kindly. The leader invited us to tune in to the present moment and name what we were feeling. Several students spoke with warmth: they felt safe, connected, open. Then one participant, a white woman, said she did not feel safe and was struggling to be vulnerable.

In an instant, something inside me shut down. My body stiffened, my breath grew shallow, and a wave of panic pressed against my chest. It was not the panic that screams; it was the panic that freezes. Her words landed on me like a weight. She had not said my name, but I felt implicated. Because I knew what happens in this country when white women do not feel safe. My body knew that story long before my mind could process it.

My first impulse was not curiosity or compassion. It was responsibility. Without thinking, I leaned forward, softened my tone, and tried to reassure her. I rushed to make the space comfortable for her, to carry the burden of her unease. It was automatic, the reflex of someone who has spent a lifetime trying to be safe for others. The Black woman who does not disrupt. The one who soothes. The one who absorbs discomfort so no one else has to. The one who smiles even when she wants to cry.

Another group member noticed what was happening and gently said, "It sounds like you feel responsible for her feeling unsafe." That simple reflection cracked something open in me. A flood of words poured out. I admitted to the group that her statement had triggered something deep. I confessed that when she said she did not feel safe, I immediately thought about the history written on my body—the consequences that follow when white women say they feel unsafe. I had not planned to say any of it, but the truth rose up unfiltered, raw, and impossible to hold back.

With the truth came tears. Hot, unwelcome tears that betrayed the composure I wanted to keep. Tears I did not want to shed in front of her, in front of anyone I had already decided I could not fully trust. Yet there they were, carving their own testimony down my face. I felt exposed, embarrassed, and furious with myself for being so vulnerable in a space that suddenly felt uneven.

The leader of the group invited us to stay with the discomfort, to name what was present, to sit in it together. But I was not ready. My defenses shot back up. I wiped my tears and insisted I did not want to talk about it anymore. What I needed was protection. What I needed was space. And more than anything, I needed someone else to hold the tension for once instead of expecting me to carry it.

In that moment, the language that came to me was "pit vipers." That is what it felt like in the room—an atmosphere thick with invisible threats that could strike without warning, leaving me poisoned, unwelcome, and unsafe. I had spent much of my life neutralizing other people's pit vipers, pretending they were not there, absorbing their venom so that no one else would be unsettled. I believed it was my job to keep the room calm, even if it meant losing myself in the process.

But in the middle of my spiraling, the Spirit whispered: You do not have to slay her pit vipers. For the first time, I let them fall to the ground. I imagined them turning to sand at my feet, powerless. I realized I had been swallowing the venom of white discomfort for far too long. That day, I decided to lay it down.

Even with that release, I was still confronted. The same participant who had spoken about not feeling safe turned to me and asked, "Why are you willing to fight my pit vipers but not release your own into the circle?"

Her question startled me. It struck at a tender place I had not touched before. The truth was painful: I did not know if I was worth that kind of care. I did not know if my pain could take up space in the circle. I did not know how to be anything other than the strong one, the spiritual one, the one who understood and made room for everyone else. I did not know how to believe that I could bring my full, unfiltered self into community and still be loved.

That day, something shifted. I began to name the burden I had carried since childhood—the belief that belonging had to be earned through usefulness, accommodation, and self-erasure. I began to see that what I thought was empathy was often reenactment of trauma. And I began to understand that true healing would require me not just to carry others' discomfort, but to let my own be seen. To stop swallowing poison. To stop trying to be safe, and to start being whole.

What Was Ours, What Was Stolen, and the Irony of Its Return

Part of decentering white culture is learning to see how it disguises itself. It renames what already existed, repackages what was sacred to us, and resells it as something new. It condemns our ways as primitive, superstitious, or shameful—until someone white adopts them. Then, suddenly, they are celebrated as innovative, profitable, or enlightened. This is not just cultural borrowing. It is theft. It is distortion. And when we begin to name what was stolen, we begin to see the water for what it is.

To name what was stolen is to remember that our practices were never broken. They were dismissed, criminalized, or hidden away, but they remained whole. They carried wisdom, survival, and spirit. They endured in us. Still do.

Here are just a few examples:

Spiritual Practices: From Ancestor Veneration to "Mindfulness"

In West African and diasporic traditions, honoring the ancestors was part of their worldview. Altars, prayers, and rituals connected us to the unseen world. These practices were not sinister—they were sacred. They were proof that our ancestors had a connection to Spirit. Under slavery and colonization, though, they were demonized. We were told that to honor our lineage in any form was to consort with darkness. Yet today, "mindfulness," "manifestation," and "meditation" flourish in Western spaces, often scrubbed of African influence.

Modern irony: A Black woman lighting a candle on an altar may be rebuked in church, while a white influencer holding crystals earns a book deal.

Rhythmic Expression: From Drumming to "Music Therapy"

Our drums were outlawed because they carried power. In 1740, the Negro Act in South Carolina banned drumming, out of fear that rhythm itself could spark rebellion. And perhaps it could. Drums were more than instruments—they were language. They called people home, carried grief, and ushered praise. They were a lifeline to Africa. Yet now, rhythm and percussion are praised in music therapy and education, packaged as innovation.

Modern irony: What once got us punished is now sold in workshops and textbooks.

Herbal Healing: From Hoodoo to "Holistic Wellness"

Our grandmothers knew how to heal. They made poultices that pulled infection, boiled roots for coughs, and whispered prayers over herbs. Their practices were dismissed as "old wives' tales," mocked as superstition, and in some cases criminalized as witchcraft. Black midwives and root women were driven underground. Yet now, white wellness entrepreneurs run apothecaries, selling herbal tinctures and oils at high prices.

Modern irony: What was once ridiculed as backwards now earns six-figure sponsorships.

Music and Dance: From Ring Shouts to Pop Stardom

We danced with our whole selves—spirit, sweat, and soul. From ring shouts to gospel hollers, from juke joints to block parties, our movement was protest, prayer, and praise. We were told our music was vulgar, our hips too loose, our rhythms too wild. Yet generations of white artists have built careers mimicking our sound.

Modern irony: Our music was "unholy" until it became profitable.

Language: From African Vernaculars to AAVE to TikTok Trends

From survival, we created a language. African American Vernacular English (AAVE) is a linguistic masterpiece, blending African syntax, Southern rhythm, and coded resilience. For generations, it was shamed as ignorant, uneducated speech. Yet today, social media and brands thrive on our slang.

Modern irony: A Black child is corrected for saying "periodt" in school while corporations sell T-shirts with the same word.

Beauty: From Natural Bodies to Cosmetic Trends

Our lips, hips, hair, and skin were ridiculed for centuries. We were told we had to straighten, lighten, and shrink to be acceptable. Yet today, the same features are praised when displayed on non-Black bodies.

Modern irony: A Black girl is suspended for wearing box braids while a white pop star is praised on magazine covers for the same style.

These examples could continue endlessly. But the truth is not only in what was stolen. The deeper truth is in what survived. Our ways did not vanish. They were tucked into whispers, carried in recipes, woven into rhythm, spoken in coded language. They live on in us—in our DNA, in our laughter, in our dreams. They remain sacred, even when the world refuses to name them as such.

Naming what was stolen is painful, because it means acknowledging not only what was taken from us, but what we sometimes gave away to survive. We softened our voices, straightened our hair, muted our worship, and tucked away our traditions. Not out of shame, but out of necessity. Survival required sacrifice, and many of us paid that price.

But survival is not the end of the story. Survival was the bridge. What lies beyond is a return. A remembering. A reclaiming of what has always been ours.

From Cultural Theft to Coming Home

Assimilation is not only about how we speak, dress, or style our hair. It is about what we forget. Slowly, subtly, we forget the rhythms that once grounded us. We forget the roots that once guided us. We forget the ways we once knew ourselves as whole. It happens quietly, under the guise of survival, until one day we look in the mirror and realize that parts of us have been traded away in the name of belonging.

I am not trying to romanticize a past that we have been disconnected from. Not every element of African spirituality aligns with what Bible-believing Christians hold as truth, and we honor God by acknowledging that. Yet within those ancient practices are echoes—embodied rhythms, communal rituals, ways of knowing—that remind us we were made for connection, not erasure. Coming home is not about taking on everything our ancestors carried; it is about discerning, with Scripture and Spirit, what is life-giving and what reflects the *Imago Dei*.

For much of my life, I did not recognize that I was assimilating. I thought I was simply doing what was necessary to succeed. I believed the messages I had absorbed: that intelligence required polish, that dignity meant restraint, that credibility required me to sound a certain way. I thought that in order to be taken seriously, I needed to sand down my edges, soften my truth, and package my passion in a way that would not feel threatening. I thought I was climbing the ladder, when in fact I was losing pieces of my soul along the way.

I did not hate being Black. But I did hate the signs of my Blackness that drew disapproval. My hair, for example. When I was a child, I longed for loose curls. I begged for a Carefree Curl because I thought that look was closer to what was acceptable. I did not understand that the texture I was trying to create was already mine, just buried beneath years of chemicals and shame. It was not until I did a "big chop" years later that I discovered the beauty that had been there all along. I realized I had spent years torturing my hair to imitate what God had already given me freely.

The same pattern showed up in my writing, even in this very book. I caught myself trying to sound academic, layering on explanations, softening the sharpness of my convictions. I was tempted to make my testimony read like a textbook. Why? Because I thought if I didn't sound professorial, I wouldn't be taken seriously. I thought my truth had to be dressed up in citations to be worthy of being heard. But deep down, I knew that wasn't true. I knew I was not called to translate my story into the language of systems that never valued my ancestors in the first place.

That is the cost of assimilation. It offers access, but only in exchange for authenticity. It hands you a seat at the table while requiring you to starve parts of yourself in silence. And at the end of the day, the seat is never secure. It can be pulled out from under you at any moment, leaving you hollow and unrooted.

But here is the grace: we can come home. We can choose to stop measuring ourselves against standards that were never ours. We can release the need to be palatable. We can step back into our cadence, our rhythm, our joy, and our faith. We can name what we lost, grieve it, and return to the truth that never left us.

Even when we forgot, God did not forget. Even when we tried to disappear into the mold, God kept us in remembrance. What God placed in us—our creativity, our emotion, our communal instinct, our sacred imagination—was never meant to be erased. It was meant to be lived. It was meant to testify. It was meant to shine.

Coming home does not mean recreating the past exactly as it was. It means reconnecting with the wisdom that was always alive in us. It means honoring the parts of ourselves that carry ancestral strength, even when we tried to bury them. It means trusting that we do not need to assimilate to be whole, to be brilliant, to be worthy of love and dignity. It means remembering that we already are.

Reclaiming Worth and Embracing Foreign Citizenship

There comes a moment in every healing journey when the world no longer feels the same. Rooms that once felt like honors to enter start to feel too small. Standards that once seemed aspirational now appear constricting. Invitations that once made us feel chosen begin to feel like compromises. This is not arrogance. This is awakening. When your eyes open to the water you have been swimming in, you stop twisting yourself to fit its currents.

Awakening brings clarity. It reminds you that you were never created to be small, muted, or invisible. It reminds you that you were never meant to measure yourself by values that deny your essence. You begin to see that survival, while sacred, was only part of the story. Thriving requires something more: a reclamation of worth.

Reclaiming worth means choosing not to contort yourself into someone else's mold. It means refusing to shrink your laughter, your voice, your rhythm, or your prayers to make others more comfortable. It means recognizing that you are not broken, that you never were. It means daring to believe that your dignity does not rise or fall with your proximity to whiteness.

This shift feels like living in a foreign land. You speak the language, but the values do not belong to you. You can navigate the system, but you never feel fully at home in it. This is the paradox of Black life in America: we are fully American and yet always aware of being othered. To awaken is to finally name that tension without shame.

Living as a foreign citizen in this way is not rejection of America. It is refusal to be erased within it. It is the awareness that our belonging is deeper than any flag or border. We are rooted in something larger. We are descendants of survivors who carried memory, faith, and rhythm across oceans. We are covenant people, connected to God and to one another in ways no system can erase.

Romans 11 speaks of being "grafted in" — of once being a wild olive shoot, now sharing in the nourishing root of something cultivated. Paul was writing to Gentile believers, reminding them that their inclusion in the family of God wasn't a mistake or an afterthought.

They belonged. And so do we.

Even when the family tree is fractured. Even when the records are gone. Even when all you have is one name and the weight of what was lost. In Christ, we are not rootless. We are grafted in, joined into God's love, God's promise, and God's people. We are part of a holy lineage.

To reclaim our worth is to return to this truth. We belong to each other, to our ancestors, to God. Our roots stretch deeper than national identity, deeper than the myths of whiteness. And in that truth, we find freedom. We are no longer bound by the need to prove ourselves to systems never meant to honor us.

This reclamation also asks us to embrace the discomfort we sometimes feel in spaces that call themselves home but are not truly hospitable. That discomfort is not delusion; it is discernment. It is the Spirit's reminder that we were created for more. It is an inner knowing that our lives cannot be contained by narratives that were never written for our thriving.

And here is the gift: once you stop striving to belong where you were never meant to fit, you can finally come home to yourself. You no longer wait for permission to take up space. You no longer beg for affirmation that was already spoken over you by God. You stand in the truth that you are fearfully and wonderfully made.

You do not have to earn your seat at the table. You are the table. You do not have to copy someone else's light. You are the fire. You do not have to contort yourself for acceptance. You already carry divine affirmation, and that is enough.

A Word About Allies

Before closing this chapter, I want to speak directly about those who walk beside us—those who are not Black yet choose to stand in solidarity, with humility and respect. Allies are often spoken about in abstract terms, but for me, this is personal. My own husband is white, with family roots in Italy, and he has been one of my fiercest protectors. To use the vernacular, he don't play about me. He is my biggest fan, my steady provider, the one who makes it his business to care for me, celebrate me, and create comfort in my life. He does not shy away from my Blackness—he honors it, loves it, and lifts it up. In fact, if I am honest, there have been times when he has lovingly pointed out places where I was still carrying internalized white supremacy, encouraging me to lean even more fully into my Blackness. That kind of allyship is not fragile. It is faithful. It does not demand the spotlight. It helps me shine more brightly in my own light.

I have also seen this in other allies. One of them is my therapist, a blue-eyed man who has never once made me feel like I had to teach in order to be heard. He does not posture as an expert on my lived experience. Instead, he listens with care, acknowledges what he cannot know, and consistently holds space without centering himself. That is allyship.

True allyship is not performative. It does not demand constant reassurance or gratitude. It does not require a seat at the table we built. It shows up with respect. It listens more than it speaks. It takes responsibility rather than shifting the burden. And sometimes, it even risks the comfort of other white people to stand in solidarity with us.

I want to say this with both care and clarity: this book was not written to explain Blackness to white people. Its purpose is to center the emotional, cultural, and spiritual journey of Black women who have lived too long on the margins of dominant culture. If reading these words makes some white readers uncomfortable, that discomfort is not rejection. It is an invitation. An invitation to see the water. To recognize that neutrality was never neutral. To ask themselves whose comfort has been prioritized, and at what cost.

I am grateful for allies who understand this, who do not need to be coddled, who speak up even when it costs them, who know that the work is not only interpersonal but also internal. I am blessed to share my life with a man who embodies that posture of protection, love, and truth-telling. And I am strengthened by knowing there are others who practice allyship with that same spirit of humility.

The louder you live in your truth, the safer I feel to live in mine. And when allies walk faithfully, without centering themselves, they make more room for all of us to breathe, to rest, and to be free.

The Truth That Remains

This chapter has been about naming the water we have been swimming in, the cultural currents that told us to shrink, the lies that framed whiteness as the only standard, the burdens that demanded our silence, and the pieces of ourselves we learned to tuck away. We have looked directly at the myths, the theft, and the toll of trying to belong in spaces never designed to hold us in our fullness.

But healing is not only about leaving behind what wounded us. Healing is also about returning. Returning to the sounds, the practices, and the truths that never died within us. Returning to the spiritual inheritance that whispered in our grandmother's prayers, pulsed in the rhythm of our music, and endured in our laughter even through tears. Returning to the God who never required us to erase our Blackness in order to be holy.

When we reclaim our worth, we are not rejecting faith, we are remembering it. We are remembering that our ancestors sang songs of deliverance even when chains rattled around them. We are remembering that our bodies, our voices, and our rhythms carry sacred memory. We are remembering that God's glory shines in us as we are, not as whiteness told us we had to be. God never called whiteness the measure of holiness. God never demanded that we trade our soul for acceptance.

We are stepping into a new posture. No longer bending to fit into cramped spaces, no longer apologizing for being too much, no longer questioning if we are enough. We are embracing radiance. Because once you see the water, you no longer swim blindly in it. You learn to move differently. You learn to claim your own reflection.

And that reflection is not distorted. It is not diminished. It is divine.

So as we leave this chapter, I want to remind you: you are not broken, you are not too much, and you are not invisible. You are the table, the fire, and the testimony. You carry the image of God in your being, and that truth is unshakable.

The systems around us may still cling to white-centered values, but we no longer have to. Not in our hearts. Not in our homes. Not in our healing. The next chapter is about seeing our reflection in the water—clear, sacred, and whole. We will look not just at what has been taken from us, but at what has been preserved in us all along.

Because when we begin to see ourselves rightly, we begin to walk in the truth that we were never meant to be small. We were meant to shine with the brilliance of God's glory.

CHAPTER 8

The *Imago Dei*

It was quiet when I sat down to write. Not the kind of silence that feels empty, but the kind that feels full—like somebody's watching, waiting. I lit a candle, opened my journal, and tried to find the words for this next chapter. That's when I felt her again. Mama Feely. Not with thunder or fanfare, but with that steady presence I've come to know. That warmth. That wisdom. That way she has of showing up when I'm wrestling with something deep.

I imagined her sitting across from me, her lap full of folded hands, her eyes kind but steady. And in my spirit, I heard her speak:

> *"Mmm-hmm. I knew you'd get here. Took your time, but you here now.*
>
> *Baby, before dey told you who you was—God already done named you.*
>
> *Before the whippin's, b'fo the laws, 'fore the churches that made you feel small—God done claimed you.*
>
> *You out here lookin' for yo'self in dey books, dey rules, dey ways of prayin'.*
>
> *But your name ben in God's mouth since 'fore time even got to runnin'.*
>
> *Ain't nothin' 'bout you accidental. Dat skin? Dem hips? Dat bold laugh you try to quiet down? All dat carry de mark of de Most High.*
>
> *Dey tried to make you think you too loud, too Black, too much.*
>
> *But listen to me good, now—*
>
> *You ain't never been too much for God.*
>
> *You His idea.*
>
> *Don't you shrink for nobody tryin' to make God small 'nuff to fit in dey pocket.*
>
> *'Cause baby, He big 'nuff to hold you. Just as you is."*

I stopped writing. Sat still. Let it wash over me. Because somewhere along the way, I had swallowed the lie that God only looked like 25 minute sermons, hymns with 5 stanzas, and quiet services. I thought my joy was too loud. My worship too wild. My voice too much. My expression of devotion too messy.

But Mama Feely reminded me that God's image is bigger than what we've been told. Wider. Deeper. Blacker. More tender.

So I keep writing, not just with my pen, but with my whole self—my history, my healing, my hallelujahs. And I invite you to do the same.

This chapter follows a simple arc: our identity in God's image, how that truth was distorted, and how we can recover it. We're going to remember, not just what happened to us, but who we are beneath it all. We're going to talk about the *Imago Dei*—what it means to have the imprint of the Divine within us. To reflect the Creator not despite our Blackness, but through it. To see our culture, our joy, our expression of faith as sacred.

This is the part of the journey where we don't just look back. We look in. And in doing so, we look up.

Let's begin.

The *Imago Dei* – God's Image in Every Human Being

The *Imago Dei* is a Latin phrase meaning "image of God," and it comes directly from Scripture—Genesis 1:26–27, where God says, *"Let us make humankind in our image, according to our likeness. "* These aren't just poetic words. This truth is foundational to how we understand our identity, dignity, and purpose. Before we were anything else—before our names were written in census records or our bodies counted on auction blocks—we were made in the image of the Divine.

That means your worth isn't something you have to earn. It's not dependent on your productivity, your pedigree, your pain, or your past. Your value doesn't come from how closely you can imitate whiteness, respectability, or anyone else's version of "good." It was already spoken over you at the beginning: You are made in the image of God.

The *Imago Dei* means you reflect God's character—His creativity, His compassion, His capacity for love, justice, and relationship. It doesn't mean we are God, but that we bear His likeness. It's stamped into our spiritual DNA. And yes, that includes your skin. Your culture. Your voice. Your very existence is evidence of God's artistry and intention.

But let's be honest. For many of us, this truth hasn't always felt accessible. When the theology handed down to you was filtered through colonization, white supremacy, and patriarchy, it's hard to believe that you could ever fully reflect the Divine. When you're taught to associate godliness with whiteness, stillness, and control, you may begin to wonder if there's room for your rhythm, your story, your way of worshiping.

This is why recognizing the *Imago Dei* is not just about doctrine—it's about healing. Reclaiming this truth is a radical act of spiritual resistance. It pushes back against every lie that said you were less than, too much, or unworthy. It calls you back to the original blessing: **You were made good.**

Not perfect. Not polished. Not performative.

Good.

God saw you and called it good. That's the foundation of this chapter.

God's Image in Every Human Being

It's a short phrase with deep roots—Latin for "the image of God." We find it right at the beginning of the Bible, where the foundation of our identity is laid:

> *"Then God said, 'Let us make humankind in our image, after our likeness...' So God created humankind in his image, in the image of God he created them; male and female he created them."*
> — Genesis 1:26–27 (NRSV)

That one sentence carries a profound truth: before you were anything else—before race, gender, trauma, or titles—you were imprinted with the very likeness of the Divine.

This isn't just poetic—it's powerful.

It means that every person, regardless of background, class, or skin tone, carries sacred value. You are not an afterthought. You're not disposable. You're not broken beyond repair. You are inherently worthy because the breath of God lives in you.

> *"The Spirit of God has made me, and the breath of the Almighty gives me life."*

— Job 33:4

But here's where it gets tender: many of us were not raised to believe that.

Especially if you're a Black woman in America. Especially if your people came through the brutal legacy of slavery. Especially if your brilliance has always been measured against a false standard, one that never reflected the fullness of your humanity.

Maybe you've heard the phrase "made in God's image," but never saw anyone who looked like you in stained glass or Sunday School books. Maybe you learned to associate godliness with whiteness, with quiet suffering, or with a kind of holiness that never made room for your story.

But that's not the God of Scripture.

> *"For we are what he has made us, created in Christ Jesus for good works, which God prepared beforehand to be our way of life."*
> — Ephesians 2:10

God's image is reflected in the vast, beautiful variety of humanity—different tongues, textures, skin shades, and stories. That means your full self, as a Black woman shaped by both hardship and hope, bears the fingerprint of the Divine.

That includes your hair. Your hips. Your rhythm. Your righteous rage. Your joy. Your voice.

None of that disqualifies you from holiness. It proves your sacredness.

Understanding the *Imago Dei* is not about striving to be like God through perfectionism. It's about returning to what's already true: God made you on purpose. God called you good.

> *"I praise you, for I am fearfully and wonderfully made. Wonderful are your works; that I know very well."*
>
> — Psalm 139:14

This isn't just theology—it's a healing truth.

For those of us carrying Complex PTSD, religious trauma, or generational shame, recognizing the *Imago Dei* is an act of liberation. It's how we begin to silence the lies that told us we were too much, not enough, or somehow unworthy of God's favor.

> *"You are altogether beautiful, my love; there is no flaw in you."*
>
> — Song of Songs 4:7

As a poetic affirmation, this verse reminds us of God's delight in our wholeness. So if no one's ever told you before, let me tell you now:

You were made in the image of God.

Not in spite of your Blackness. Not in spite of your history. Not in spite of your wounds.

But through them. With them. Because of them.

You bear God's image.

And that changes everything.

The Historical Disruption of Divine Identity

If we are all made in the image of God, how did we come to believe that some images are more divine than others?

For Black people in America, especially Black women, the truth of the *Imago Dei* has been under constant assault. From the moment the first African was forced onto a slave ship, stripped of language, name, land, and kin, that sacred identity was targeted. Not by accident, but by design.

Slavery didn't just steal labor, it stole identity. It didn't just chain bodies, it tried to erase the divine imprint within those bodies. White supremacy couldn't function if enslaved people were fully seen as image-bearers of God. The entire system depended on the dehumanization of Black bodies. You can't justify buying, selling, breeding, and brutalizing a person if you believe they are sacred. So something had to give—and it wasn't going to be power or money.

So a new theology was constructed.

Not from divine revelation, but from manipulation. It reimagined God in the image of the oppressor and reinterpreted Scripture to serve economic and racial domination. Whiteness was equated with godliness. Casting it as civilized, rational, and pure. Blackness was cast as cursed, savage, and subhuman. From plantation catechisms to the misuse of Genesis 9's 'Curse of Ham,' theology was often weaponized to justify slavery. Entire sermons were preached to convince slaveholders and slaves alike that bondage was part of God's will. That obedience to masters would be rewarded in heaven. That suffering in silence was holiness.

This wasn't just bad theology—it was weaponized theology.

 And it did more than control behavior. It distorted identity.

This is distortion at work; once the pulpit echoed the auction block, the sacred became suspect. Scripture was no longer a source of liberation, it became a tool of oppression. The same Bible that speaks of freedom, deliverance, and divine love was used to reinforce chains, crush resistance, and convince generations of Black people that they were spiritually inferior.

And the silence? That was part of it, too.

A refusal to name injustice.

A selective reading of the gospel.

A church that claimed to love Jesus but wouldn't sit beside His wounded children.

This distorted theology wasn't just about religion. It seeped into education, art, economics, law, and family structures. It shaped how the world saw us, and in many cases, how we came to see ourselves.

But let's be clear: this was never God's design.

It was man-made. Profit-driven. Fear-fueled.

And yet, through it all, the *Imago Dei* in Black folks remained.

Buried, maybe. Distorted, yes. But never erased.

Our ancestors knew this in their bones. Even when everything around them screamed otherwise, they still found ways to hold on to the God who sees. They saw past the lies preached from plantation pulpits. They recognized the difference between the God of the slaveholder and the God of the Exodus.

So they created hush harbors—hidden places in the woods where they could worship in freedom, away from the ears of their enslavers. There, they moaned their grief. They danced their prayers. They cried out to a God who delivered Daniel, parted the Red Sea, and heard the blood of Abel crying from the ground.

And they sang.

Spirituals weren't just songs—they were coded sermons. Testimonies wrapped in melody. Laments and longings braided with hope.

"Didn't my Lord deliver Daniel? And why not every man?"
"Swing low, sweet chariot, coming for to carry me home."
"Go down, Moses, way down in Egypt land... tell ol' Pharaoh to let my people go."

These songs were not weak cries for heaven, they were bold declarations that they were still seen by God. That they knew who they were. That their dignity had not been destroyed. In every note, they reclaimed the *Imago Dei*.

Even in the valley of the shadow of death, our ancestors created a faith that was honest, embodied, and free. A faith that said: We are still here. We are still His.

That legacy lives on in us.

"We had no song books. Everything was by ear and by memory. We would slip away to de woods and have church, like we wanted it... Dey say we couldn't have God, but dey couldn't take Him from us."

— Sarah Frances Shaw Graves, formerly enslaved woman, interviewed by the WPA Federal Writers' Project, 1937

Even under the lash and the law, our people carried a faith that refused to be extinguished. In hidden groves and whispered gatherings, they lifted their voices in defiance and devotion.

Traditional Negro Spiritual

"Nobody knows the trouble I've seen,
Nobody knows but Jesus.
Nobody knows the trouble I've seen,
Glory hallelujah."

These were not just songs of sorrow. They were theological affirmations. Our ancestors believed they were seen, known, and held by God—even when the world denied their humanity.

And through those moans, shouts, and tears, the image of God endured.

After emancipation, the same systems that once auctioned off our ancestors began rebranding themselves through Jim Crow laws, segregated churches, biased theology, and "respectable" Christianity. Black spiritual expression full of fire, movement, moaning, praise, and power was labeled as excessive or uncivilized. We were told to quiet our tongues, tame our emotions, and worship in ways that made others comfortable.

And when those lies show up over and over again on the news, in the classroom, in the pulpit, or in your own mirror, you start to wonder if they might be true.

That's how spiritual disconnection happens.

That's how trauma turns inward.

That's how the sacred becomes shadowed.

Many of us learned to see ourselves not as beloved, but as burdens. Not as chosen, but as tolerated. And the church did not always help. It often mirrored the same exclusionary standards we saw in the world, teaching us to draw near to God only after shrinking ourselves down to fit a mold that was never made for us.

But God never stopped seeing us.

Even in the fields.

Even in the pews where we sat unseen.

Even in the silence after our prayers went unanswered.

> *"But Zion said, 'The Lord has forsaken me, my Lord has forgotten me.'*
> *Can a woman forget her nursing child…? Even these may forget, yet I will*
> *not forget you. See, I have inscribed you on the palms of my hands."*
>
> — Isaiah 49:14–16

The historical distortion of divine identity was meant to sever us from our sacredness. But even in the deepest wounds, God left a remnant—a whisper, a warmth, a knowing. That still, small voice saying: You are mine.

And now, in our healing journey, we get to reclaim what was never truly lost. We get to call back the truth. Not just for ourselves, but for our daughters, nieces, and granddaughters. For the ones coming after who deserve to know they are holy, whole, and held.

Healing Through Recognizing the Image of God in You

For women navigating the long shadows of intergenerational trauma, spiritual disconnection, and Complex PTSD, healing often begins not with doing, but with remembering.

Not remembering the pain—we know that part all too well.

But remembering the truth beneath the pain:

You were made in the image of God.

You always were.

When trauma is constant, it changes how you see yourself. It can leave you hypervigilant, ashamed, or emotionally numb. You may begin to internalize the message that something is fundamentally wrong with you. And when those messages are reinforced by racism, sexism, family dysfunction, or even the church, it becomes easy to confuse spiritual damage with spiritual failure.

But hear this clearly: your wounds are not a reflection of your worth.

Your struggle is not proof of your unworthiness.

You are not broken beyond recognition—you are sacred beyond comprehension.

Healing happens when we return to the root of who we are, and for the believer, that root is God. Not just as Creator, but as the One who crafted you with intention, placed His image upon you, and called you very good (Genesis 1:31).

Recognizing the *Imago Dei* in yourself is more than an affirmation—it's a reclamation. It is how we begin to loosen the grip of shame. It's how we call our nervous systems back to safety. It's how we remember that our existence was never a mistake.

And it's also how we begin to reframe the narrative around our healing. You are not just trying to "get better". You are returning to the truth that was always yours. You are returning to your wholeness.

> *"You shall be called by a new name that the mouth of the Lord will give… You shall no more be termed Forsaken… but you shall be called My Delight Is in Her."*
>
> — Isaiah 62:2–4

There is profound power in knowing you bear God's image even in your woundedness. Even in your questions. Even in your exhaustion.

This isn't just spiritual language. It's soul restoration. And it's deeply practical. When you begin to see yourself as sacred, it changes how you:

- Set boundaries without guilt
- Speak up when something feels off
- Pursue therapy and healing without shame
- Worship in ways that feel honest and embodied
- Resist systems that try to make you smaller

The *Imago Dei* becomes the foundation on which you rebuild your sense of self.

And when you forget, as we all do, come back to this truth:

You are fearfully and wonderfully made. And your soul knows it even if it's been a while since you've felt it.

Cultural Expressions of Faith Are Holy Too

When we say we are made in the image of God, we often picture it as a personal truth—something individual and internal. And it is. But the *Imago Dei* is not just a private reality. It's also a communal and cultural one. You bear God's image not only in your body or your soul, but in the way you live, move, worship, grieve, and celebrate. God's image doesn't stop at your skin—it flows through your culture, your traditions, your joy, your rhythm, your way of being in the world.

This isn't just poetic—it's theological.

In **Genesis 1:26–28**, when God says, "Let us make humankind in our image," the Hebrew word for "image" (tselem) points to something both inherent and active. The image of God is not just about what we are—it's also about what we do. God blesses humankind and gives us a mandate: to create, to steward, to build life in relationship with others. This implies that our cultures—how we organize life, make meaning, express joy, honor our dead, tell stories, and gather in worship—are all part of living out the image of God in community.

Theologians like Catherine LaCugna and Willie James Jennings remind us that God is not a solitary being. God exists as Trinity—a divine community of love and relationship. So when we are made in that image, it means we reflect God not just in our personhood, but in our relationality. That includes family. That includes

163

language. That includes the ancestral recipes, the harmonies, the side-eyes that communicates everything from mother to wiggly children in church pews, and the sacred hush of shared grief. God's image is communal by design.

We also see this truth affirmed in Acts 2, on the day of Pentecost. When the Holy Spirit filled the disciples, people from every nation didn't hear the gospel in a new, unified language—they heard it in their own mother tongues. That moment wasn't just a miracle of sound, it was a miracle of cultural affirmation. God spoke to each person in the language of their heart, showing that diversity is not a problem to overcome—it's a part of God's plan.

And in Revelation 7:9, we get a glimpse of eternity. It doesn't describe a colorless, culture-less crowd. It says, "a great multitude... from every nation, from all tribes and peoples and languages" stands before the throne of God, still clothed in their uniqueness, still bearing their cultural identities. This tells us that our ethnic and cultural distinctiveness is not something to shed in order to draw closer to God, it's something we carry with us into His presence.

So when you worship with your whole body...

When you moan and shout and sing and sway...

When you tell stories passed down through generations...

When your soul reaches for God through rhythm and movement...

You are not being extra. You are being faithful.

Black folks have always related to God in ways that are embodied and expressive, born out of both suffering and strength. But too often, we've been told that those expressions are "less than." That our churches are too loud, our worship too emotional, our theology too "simple." We've been asked to leave our culture at the door in order to be seen as "spiritually mature."

But here's the truth: **God never asked you to be less Black in order to be more holy.**

Your culture is not a barrier to God—it's a window into Him.

Your way of worshiping, your spiritual memory, your sacred habits—they reflect a part of God that the world needs to see.

When you bring your full self into your faith, you're not just remembering who you are. You're revealing who God is.

Let me share a secret...

I didn't think I was bad at theology. I considered myself very familiar with the Bible. I had taught Bible studies. I had spent years immersed in Scripture, leaning on it for guidance, comfort, and direction. But when I got to seminary, I found myself in a strange and unsettling place: I kept failing the very classes that were supposed to deepen my theological understanding.

Old Testament. New Testament. I took them multiple times. These were my systematic theology courses, and no matter how much I studied or prayed, I couldn't seem to pass. I was confused—really confused. Not because I didn't know the stories or understand God's character, but because the way theology was being presented felt foreign, overly academic, and disconnected from everything I had ever known about how God moves.

Meanwhile, I got an A in Biblical Interpretation. Go figure.

That class gave me space to engage the text with curiosity, honesty, and insight. I could bring myself to it—my questions, my culture, my context. And the text came alive. But in my systematic theology classes, it felt like I had to leave all of that at the door.

It wasn't that I didn't believe in the authority of Scripture or the importance of doctrine. I just didn't understand why everything had to sound so cold—so far removed from the living, breathing God I had encountered in prayer, in worship, in the Black churches of my youth. I was wrestling with more than information. I was wrestling with form, with language, with a way of knowing God that felt closed off to the world I came from.

In my childhood churches—small, Black storefront sanctuaries that dotted the streets of inner-city Chicago—God was visceral. Church was rhythm. The Spirit was caught, not explained. And even though the sermons weren't academically trained or exegetically deep, I felt God there. In the sway of a deaconess. In the moan of a prayer warrior. In the moments of breathlessness between songs. In the joy that came from surviving another week.

No one ever told me that that was theology too.

So when I got to seminary and faced the cool precision of Western theological language, I didn't know how to translate what I carried. I had grown up in a world where the Holy Ghost made you shout, where the Word was read from the King James, where emotion was not only allowed—it was the point. But in class, I learned to flatten God into propositions and doctrines. I learned that "faithfulness" meant separating what I felt from what I believed. It was as if the God I had known in my body wasn't welcome in the classroom.

I passed eventually. But I carried disappointment—not just in myself, but in the fact that no one had ever told me there were other ways to know God. That there was room for my culture, my questions, my embodied knowing.

Looking back now, I understand the difference.

It wasn't that I lacked intelligence. It was that the God presented in my Old and New Testament courses felt foreign—filtered through Eurocentric frameworks that had no room for the God of the hush harbor. But in the Biblical Interpretation course, I was given space to engage the text as a living word. I could ask real questions, draw connections to my lived experience, and recognize the Spirit's movement in how I read. That space felt like home.

And when I finally took Advanced Theology—not for a letter grade, but just to learn—I realized I could've earned an A there too. Not because the content changed, but because I did. I had begun the sacred work of integrating what I knew in my bones with what I was learning in the academy. I had started to trust that God was not just found in the footnotes—but also in the foot-stomps and the tambourines of my youth.

I now see my faith not as one story, but as a mosaic. A holy collage made of broken academic confidence, storefront sermons, creeds I hold to, and questions I still carry. I've learned to let my ancestors sit beside the theologians. I let the Apostle's Creed stand next to my grandmother's whispered prayers. I trust that the Spirit who hovered over the waters still moves in my body, still speaks in my voice, still shows up in my story.

My faith is no longer either/or.

It's both/and.

And yours can be too. Now we turn to recovery

Implications for Missions and Church Life

If we truly believe that every person is made in the image of God, then this belief should radically change how we engage with others—especially in ministry, missions, and church leadership.

But for too long, the Church, particularly in its Western expressions, has preached the *Imago Dei* while behaving as if some images are more divine than others. Christian missions, colonization, and Western expansion often went hand in hand. Entire communities were told they had to abandon their language, customs, dress, and ways of worshiping in order to "receive the gospel." Christianity was exported alongside European cultural values, and faith became entangled with assimilation.

The result? Countless people around the world came to know Jesus while being taught—implicitly or explicitly—that their own cultures were inferior. That to be Christian meant to dress a certain way, sing a certain kind of music, speak a certain language, follow a certain leadership structure, and uphold Western norms of "order" and "decency."

This is not the gospel of Jesus Christ. This is cultural imperialism wrapped in Scripture.

> *"The thief comes only to steal and kill and destroy. I came that they may have life, and have it abundantly."*
> — John 10:10

True evangelism does not require erasure. In fact, it must resist it.

If the image of God is present in every people, then the goal of missions is not to make others more like us—it's to help each person more fully become who God created them to be. That means valuing cultural expressions of worship, leadership, family, and even theology. That means listening before speaking. Learning before leading. Being present before prescribing.

This truth also applies to church life here at home.

Some Black women, like myself, have found themselves in predominantly white church spaces where they are asked to conform to the dominant culture in order to be fully accepted. That conformity may be subtle—a change in tone, a shift in dress, a discomfort with expressive worship—or it may be explicit, with leadership structures that lack diversity and theology that fails to name racial injustice.

But if the Church is the Body of Christ, then it needs all its members functioning—not just the hands and feet that fit neatly into someone else's idea of order. The Black church, the Afro-Caribbean church, the Indigenous church, the immigrant church—these aren't side notes. They are essential to the richness and fullness of the Kingdom of God.

> *"Now there are varieties of gifts, but the same Spirit... For just as the body is one and has many members, and all the members of the body, though many, are one body—so it is with Christ."*
>
> — 1 Corinthians 12:4, 12

Decolonizing our faith doesn't mean abandoning orthodoxy. It means recognizing that orthodoxy has often been taught through a narrow lens. It means expanding our understanding of how the Holy Spirit moves—across cultures, languages, and traditions. It means honoring the divine image in people as they are, not as we prefer them to be.

The implications are clear: if we want to live in a way that truly honors the *Imago Dei* in each of us, we must make space for different ways of knowing, praising, leading, and believing. We must build churches where all parts of the Body are not only welcomed, but centered and celebrated. We must engage in missions that do not conquer, but partner—that do not impose, but invite. If we want to live in a way that honors God's image in all people, we must dismantle practices that distort it.

Because every culture carries a glimpse of God.

And every time we make room for that glimpse, we see Him more clearly.

An Invitation to Reclaim Your Spiritual Identity

By now, you've heard the truth:

You were made in the image of God.

Not in spite of your story, your culture, or your skin—but through them.

You are not missing anything. You are not spiritually defective.

You are whole. You are sacred. You are seen.

But knowing that in your head and carrying it in your heart are two different things.

So this is your invitation—not just to agree with the theology, but to live into it. To begin reclaiming your spiritual identity not as an intellectual exercise, but as an act of healing. As an act of resistance. As a return to the you that God has always known and loved.

You don't have to do it all at once. But you can start here:

Notice the moments when you feel the need to shrink. Ask yourself, Who taught me I had to do this to belong?

- **Remember** the times when your body knew God was present, even if theology didn't explain it.
- **Explore** spiritual expressions from your heritage that were once dismissed as "too much" or "not biblical."

- **Trust** the Spirit within you to guide you into deeper truth, not just through books but through experience, memory, and presence.

Your spirituality doesn't have to fit in someone else's frame. It was never meant to.

Maybe your prayers don't sound like the ones you were taught. Maybe your worship comes through your body, through dance or moans or stillness. Maybe you hear God best in music, or in movement, or in the hush of early morning.

That's not irreverent. That's real.

> *"For freedom Christ has set us free. Stand firm, therefore, and do not submit again to a yoke of slavery."*
> — Galatians 5:1

The beauty of reclaiming your spiritual identity is that it doesn't require you to erase anything—it invites you to integrate everything. In my case, that integration includes the child who sat in storefront churches, the student who wrestled in seminary, the woman who leads and learns and cries and prays today. Like me, every part of you is welcome at the altar.

You don't have to mimic someone else's path to find God. You just have to remember your own.

So, beloved, come home to yourself. Come home to the God who formed you, who walks with you, who delights in the sound of your voice and the shape of your worship.

You are not an outsider looking in. You are an image-bearer. A daughter. A reflection of glory. Next, we'll practice re-training body and spirit to live from this truth of the *Imago Dei.*

God of our becoming,

You who formed us in Your image and called us good—

Thank You for the truth that we are fearfully and wonderfully made.

Thank You for every thread of culture, story, memory, and song that reflects Your beauty through us.

Forgive us for the times we believed we were too much—or not enough.

For the ways we shrank to fit into spaces that couldn't hold our fullness.

For the parts of Your likeness in ourselves we hid to survive.

Today, we reclaim what was always ours.

Our voice.

Our rhythm.

Our way of knowing You.

Our right to worship with all that we are.

Spirit of Truth, dwell with us in every breath.

Help us to see ourselves through Your eyes and to hold fast to the truth that our Blackness is not a burden but a blessing.

That our spiritual journey—rooted in faith, forged in fire—is sacred ground.

Lead us from shame to wholeness, from fragmentation to flourishing, from silence to testimony.

And as we move into the work of healing, be our strength, our guide, and our steady place to land.

We are Yours.

Fully. Freely. Forever.

Amen.

Part 3: Healing

CHAPTER 9

Faith and Resilience

The *Imago Dei* and the Gift of Resilience

When we see ourselves as bearers of God's image, it reframes how we understand our worth, our suffering, and our capacity to endure. The *Imago Dei* is not erased by trauma or hardship. It remains intact, even when life tries to convince us otherwise. And it is from this place of divine identity that resilience begins to grow.

Think back to Tiana, whom we met in the introduction. Behind the steering wheel, her hands tight and trembling, she had been swept up in rage and then consumed by shame, asking herself why she couldn't "just stay calm." In that moment, Tiana felt the full weight of being pressed on every side, struggling with emotions that seemed too heavy to carry.

Her blow-up with her sister was about much more than the question of who should check on Mama. It was about everything that had been simmering beneath the surface: the exhaustion of holding down a demanding job while still feeling invisible at work, the quiet grief of watching bills outpace her paycheck, the responsibility of being the one everyone in the family depends on, and the loneliness of raising children with little support. Add to that the ache of past wounds she never had space to process, and it becomes clear. Her outburst was not random. It was the overflow of compounded pressure. With no safe outlet for grief, anger, or exhaustion, the pressure had nowhere to go but outward.

Do Tiana's struggles feel familiar? They reflect the tensions so many of us hold inside: anger and grief, love and frustration, faith and doubt, all colliding at once.

Too often, resilience is described as "bouncing back," as if we simply snap into place after life has bent us out of shape. But resilience is deeper than that. It is not about pretending we are unbreakable, it is about knowing where our true anchor lies. Resilience is the sacred tether that keeps us from drifting into despair when the storms rage. It is less about our ability to push through on our own and more about being rooted in Someone greater than ourselves. Resilience doesn't erase grief; it enables endurance with integrity.

The Apostle Paul captured this mystery in his letter to the Corinthians: "We are hard pressed on every side, but not crushed; perplexed, but not in despair; persecuted, but not abandoned; struck down, but not destroyed" (2 Corinthians 4:8-9). These words remind us that resilience is not the absence of struggle. It is the presence of God's sustaining power in the midst of it. This chapter will explore how faith in Jesus Christ becomes the wellspring of resilience, equipping us to carry both our wounds and our hope, knowing that we are never alone.

Understanding Resilience in Trauma and Healing

Resilience is one of those words that gets used often but not always understood. In psychological terms, resilience is the capacity to adapt positively in the face of adversity, to navigate hardship without being undone by it. It doesn't mean life is easy, or that we are untouched by pain. Instead, resilience is the set of internal and external resources that allow us to withstand pressure and recover a sense of stability, even when circumstances remain difficult.

But if resilience is so critical, why does it sometimes feel like some people have it in abundance while others can barely hold on? Part of the answer lies in what psychologists call protective factors. These are the buffers that soften the blow of life's hardships. A strong support system, a sense of belonging in community, healthy coping strategies, and—for many of us—faith, all serve as anchors. When these factors are present, they provide scaffolding for us to lean on.

Yet not everyone has access to such scaffolding. Some of us grew up in homes or communities where trauma was ongoing and relentless. Others carry the weight of systemic oppression—racism, sexism, classism—that cuts off opportunities for healing. Chronic stress, isolation, and lack of resources can strip away the very buffers we need most. Without them, resilience becomes harder to access, not because someone is weak or broken, but because the ground beneath them has been eroded.

This is where emotional literacy becomes essential. As Brené Brown points out in Atlas of the Heart, most people can only name four or five feelings—usually happy, sad, mad, tired, or anxious. But our emotional landscape is far more nuanced than that. When we don't have the words, we often don't have the awareness we need to process our feelings. Rage might really be grief. Numbness might actually be fear. Irritability might be deep loneliness. Without language, emotions stay muddled, and muddled emotions often spill out sideways.

That's why I often use a feelings wheel with clients. A feelings wheel is a simple circular chart that begins with broad emotional categories (like anger, joy, sadness, or fear) at its center and branches outward into more precise, layered emotions. For example, "anger" might expand into "frustrated," "jealous," or "resentful," each carrying a different shade of experience. Clients can point to what resonates with them in the moment, sometimes discovering emotions they didn't realize they were carrying. This tool can be found easily online. Many versions are free to download and print, and therapists often keep a laminated copy in their offices. Simply googling "feelings wheel" will yield several helpful options. The goal isn't to memorize every word on the wheel, but to build curiosity and expand the language of the heart.

From a clinical perspective, resilience requires buffers. Trauma strips away those buffers, leaving us exposed to every new blow without protection. But here is where faith becomes more than just belief; it becomes a living buffer. Jesus Christ, who promises never to leave nor forsake us, steps into the places where our human scaffolding has collapsed. When we lean into Him, we discover resilience that is not manufactured by sheer willpower but gifted through His presence. In other words, the buffers we may lack in the world can be reintroduced through faith, community, and the sustaining Spirit of God.

Christ as Our Buffer

One of the most powerful promises in Scripture is this: "I will never leave you nor forsake you" (Hebrews 13:5). These words matter deeply when life has stripped away the buffers we depend on. Human supports may fail us, but Christ Himself steps in as the steady presence that keeps us from collapsing under the weight of our struggles. And this assurance is not abstract—it is secured through the atonement. Because of His shed blood, we are not only forgiven but restored. What was lost to assimilation and oppression does not have the final word. The cross makes it possible to sift through what has been handed down, to reclaim what reflects God's image in us, and to release what does not. In Him, we as believers are given both the freedom and the discernment to come home to ourselves without fear of straying from Him.

Systems and history have scarred us deeply, but Scripture also reminds us that brokenness is not only 'out there.' Sin touches each human heart. This does not mean our trauma is our fault—never that. It means that just as we need healing from what has been done to us, we also need forgiveness and redemption for what we ourselves have done. The good news is that Christ, through His shed blood, makes restoration possible on both fronts: freedom from the wounds inflicted by others, and freedom from the weight of our own sin. Naming sin doesn't erase trauma. It simply reminds us that Christ redeems us fully, in every dimension of our lives.

Think again of Tiana. Her argument with her sister was only the spark; the real fire was the exhaustion of doing too much with too little support, the financial strain that never seemed to ease, and the ache of carrying old wounds she didn't have space to process. In clinical terms, she had been living without the buffers resilience requires. Instead of small, manageable stressors that could strengthen her over time, a process psychologists call stress inoculation, Tiana had endured a flood of challenges all at once. Stress inoculation works like a vaccine: by facing difficulties in safe, measured doses and practicing coping skills, we grow stronger. When stress is bounded and controllable, this works. But when the stress is relentless and unbuffered, as it often is for women like Tiana, it doesn't strengthen, it depletes.

This is where Christ makes all the difference. Christ's presence doesn't remove agency; it resources it. He is not only our companion in suffering but also our protector, the buffer who absorbs what would otherwise crush us. He doesn't prevent us from feeling the sting of sorrow or the press of responsibility, but His presence ensures that sorrow does not swallow us whole. Where trauma strips away scaffolding, faith rebuilds it through His Spirit, His promises, and His unrelenting love.

For Tiana, and for many of us, this truth reframes resilience. It is not about suppressing emotions or pretending to be strong on our own. It is about allowing Christ to stand between us and the full force of our burdens, transforming what could destroy us into testimony that He is alive within us.

Biblical Foundations of Resilience

Paul's words in 2 Corinthians 4 remind us that resilience is not about escaping hardship, but about being sustained through it. He writes that we hold "this treasure in jars of clay" (v. 7). The image is striking: we are fragile vessels—cracked, chipped, and vulnerable—yet within us rests the surpassing power of God. The very weakness of the clay becomes the stage where His strength is revealed. Our resilience doesn't come from the vessel itself but from the treasure it carries.

Paul continues with the paradox of the Christian life: we carry both death and life at the same time. "We always carry in our bodies the death of Jesus, so that the life of Jesus may also be revealed" (v. 10). Suffering is real. We carry death. But it is never the full story. In the very places where we feel broken, the life of Christ shines through. This is the heart of biblical resilience: fragility and glory, struggle and endurance, existing side by side.

This theological truth has been lived out generation after generation in the Black church. As researchers C. Eric Lincoln and Lawrence Mamiya observed, the Black church became the central space where African Americans held both lament and hope at the same time. It was, and still is, a place where jars of clay are reminded of the treasure within, and where believers testify that "trouble don't last always."

For someone like Tiana, this legacy is daily lived out as a survival strategy. After her blow-up with her sister, imagine her walking into her church on a weary Sunday morning. She comes in heavy, still ashamed of the words she shouted, still weighed down by unpaid bills and the endless cycle of caretaking. But before she can even sit down, an usher squeezes her hand and says, "Glad to see you this morning, baby." In that moment, she remembers she belongs.

The choir begins to sing, voices rising with the familiar refrain of a hymn passed down through generations: "God will take care of you." As tears sting her eyes, Tiana realizes she doesn't have to hold it all together alone. A sister in the pew leans over and whispers, "You gon' be alright." The pastor proclaims, echoing Paul, "You may feel pressed, but you're not crushed." God is still with you." The words land like a balm. For that hour, the sanctuary becomes her buffer, absorbing some of the weight, reframing her shame, reminding her that Christ's life is still at work in her fragile vessel.

This is what Lincoln and Mamiya described in their research: the Black church as both a spiritual refuge and a wellspring of resilience. For centuries, it has been the communal witness that suffering is not the end. For Tiana, and for so many like her, the church is where the theology of Paul meets the lived reality of God's people. It is where the Spirit renews us day by day, not in theory, but in song, in testimony, in prayer, in the simple act of showing up and being held.

The same Spirit that sustained our ancestors in slavery and segregation is alive in us today. And through the body of Christ gathered in community, resilience becomes not just possible, but inevitable.

The Black Church and Communal Resilience

The Black church has always been more than a place of worship. Historically, it was the survival ground for our people. A space where faith and resistance were braided together. In slavery times, it was the hush harbor, where prayers whispered in the dark became songs of freedom. During Jim Crow, it was the gathering place where courage was fed, strategies were planned, and hope was kept alive. At its core, the Black church has always been both spiritual refuge and social engine, nurturing the soul while equipping the body for the long struggle ahead.

For someone like Tiana, that history lives on every time she shows up on Sunday. When she bows her head in prayer, she is not just speaking her own words, she is joining a chorus of prayers that have carried generations through captivity, lynching, and civil rights marches. When she listens to her pastor's sermon, she is hearing more than encouragement, she is being rooted in a preaching tradition that has always named suffering while declaring God's power to sustain. And when she lifts her voice in song, she taps into the resilience woven into spirituals, gospel hymns, and praise anthems that once gave enslaved people the strength to endure another day.

Scholars remind us that African American spirituality has always integrated resilience through these practices you may know well: prayer that heals, preaching that reframes pain, music that carries lament and joy in the same breath, and community that strengthens the individual by holding them within the collective. These aren't just church traditions, they are lifelines.

Think back to Tiana's Sunday. She walked in heavy, ashamed of how she had lashed out at her sister. But when the choir lifted their voices with "God Will Take Care of You," something in her cracked open. She let her tears fall because the music made space for both her grief and her hope. Have you ever had a moment like that—when a song said what your heart couldn't find words for?

Then came the sermon. The pastor didn't dismiss the weight of her struggles; he named them. And in naming them, he reminded everyone listening that God's promises are still true. For Tiana, those words shifted the ground beneath her feet. Her shame loosened its grip. Can you picture yourself sitting in that pew, hearing a word that spoke directly to your hidden battles?

Finally, as the congregation joined hands in prayer, Tiana felt a strength she hadn't had when she walked through the door. Nothing about her situation had changed. Her bills were still waiting, her family still needed her, but she no longer carried it all by herself. That's what the Black church has always done: it holds us when we can't hold ourselves.

I want you to imagine this in your own life. What would it look like for you to allow church, the body of Christ, to be a buffer or source of resilience? Maybe it's letting a song wash over you until your shoulders unclench. Maybe it's allowing yourself to be prayed for instead of keeping it all bottled up. Maybe it's sitting still long enough to let a sermon speak to the ache you've been naming only to God.

For Tiana, that Sunday morning, her church community was the key to her survival. And it can be that for you, too.

I know this from my own journey. In the moments I felt unseen or pressed to the margins, it was the church that reminded me I still had a name, a song, and a community. It was where I learned to lament honestly and still stand in hope. And like Tiana, I found that resilience is not a solo achievement. This kind of community-supported resilience is born in the sacred spaces where God's people gather, cry, sing, and endure together.

I want to pause here and acknowledge something important: for some of you, church has not always been a safe place. Maybe you've been hurt by leaders who abused their authority, or by communities that silenced your voice instead of lifting it up. If that's part of your story, I see you. That pain is real, and it matters.

But I also want to encourage you not to give up on the possibility of spiritual community. The church, at its best, was never meant to wound—it was meant to heal. And while no congregation is perfect, there are faith communities where you can be seen, prayed for, and strengthened. Communities that remind you of your worth, hold space for your lament, and walk with you through your joy. If returning to church isn't safe, begin with a trauma-informed small group or spiritual director.

Building Resilience Through Faith Today

Resilience is not something we simply "have" or don't have—it is something we can nurture through consistent practices that strengthen us over time. Faith offers us both the spiritual foundation and the practical tools we need to endure and heal.

Trusting Christ

At its core, resilience begins with surrender. Trauma convinces us that we must control everything in order to feel safe, but faith invites us to release what we cannot carry. Trusting Christ means leaning into His promises: "I will never leave you nor forsake you." When fear and anxiety rise, resilience looks like whispering a prayer of surrender: "Lord, I can't carry this alone."

Prayer and Scripture

Prayer and Scripture are spiritual disciplines that stabilize us.   Clinically, routines help regulate our nervous systems, and spiritually, they anchor our hearts. Even short practices matter: beginning the day with a verse taped to your mirror, ending the night with one sentence of gratitude, pausing midday to whisper the Lord's Prayer. These small rhythms create guardrails when life feels chaotic.

Community

Resilience grows best in community. Trauma isolates us, convincing us we must figure things out alone. But community reconnects us to truth. Faith communities such as sister circles, Bible studies, and church gatherings become buffers that absorb life's blows and remind us we are not abandoned. Showing up, even when you feel weary or ashamed, can be an act of resilience. And if you're a single parent, resilience may feel even harder. Time, childcare, and transportation can be real barriers. But even here, God makes a way. A ten-minute check-in call, a prayer partner over the phone, or a micro-community that meets in passing moments can still become holy ground. Small practices matter, and they count.

Lament and Praise

Resilience does not mean denying pain. It means creating space for both grief and hope. The Psalms model this rhythm of lament and praise: honest cries of sorrow followed by declarations of trust. Singing through tears, praying with honesty, and lifting your voice in worship reframe suffering as something God can meet and transform. Lament empties us of what we can't hold; praise fills us with what only God can give.

Therapy Integration

Faith and therapy can work hand in hand to deepen resilience. Therapy itself can be one of the gifts God uses to bring healing. The same God who works through prayer and Scripture also works through skilled helpers, wisdom, and science. One example of how faith and therapeutic interventions can work together is the feelings wheel I mentioned earlier, an accessible tool that expands our emotional vocabulary. As most of us can only name a handful of emotions, resilience grows when we can name our feelings with more accuracy: "overwhelmed," "lonely," "disrespected," "hopeful." When integrated with prayer, those words become places of encounter with God: "Lord, meet me in my loneliness. Steady me when I feel overwhelmed." Therapy gives us language; faith gives us the assurance that no part of us is too much for God to handle.

Resilience is not about never breaking down. It is about building buffers that keep us from being destroyed when life presses in. Through trust, prayer, community, lament, praise, and the integration of faith with therapeutic tools, we create the conditions for healing—and we open ourselves to the strength of Christ alive within us.

Tiana's example

Sunday gave Tiana a breath of fresh air, but Monday morning reminded her that life was still heavy. The bills hadn't gone anywhere, the dishes still needed washing, and her phone buzzed with a text from her sister she wasn't ready to answer. Her chest tightened. The old familiar panic began to rise.

This time, though, she tried something different. She whispered, "Lord, I can't carry this alone. Help me trust You." From a therapeutic lens, this was a moment of surrender—naming what she could not control and choosing to release it. Spiritually, it was trust in action. That whisper didn't solve everything, but it softened the weight enough for her to breathe.

Later that morning, as she brushed her teeth, her eyes landed on the verse taped to the mirror: "We are pressed, but not crushed; perplexed, but not in despair." Reading those words became her daily ritual. Clinicians know that small, consistent routines regulate the nervous system, and in faith, scripture does more—it anchors the soul. That night, instead of numbing herself by scrolling on her phone until she fell asleep, Tiana prayed a short prayer of gratitude. Just one thing she could thank God for: "Thank You for giving me strength to get through today."

By midweek, Tiana's sister texted again, and the tension in her chest flared. The old script told her to isolate, to shut down in shame. But she remembered her women's small group was meeting that night. Everything in her wanted to stay home, but she pushed herself out the door. Sitting in that circle, she found the courage to say, "I've been so angry lately, and I don't know what to do with it." Instead of judgment, the women nodded, prayed, and one even offered to check in later in the week. Therapy calls this social buffering—when community absorbs the shock of life's stress—but in Tiana's experience, it felt like God Himself was reminding her she didn't have to carry her burdens alone.

On Friday, after a draining workday, she sank into her car and cranked up her gospel playlist. The first song drew tears she'd been holding back all week. She wept as she drove, lament pouring out with each mile. Then another song came on, one that made her lift her hands right there in the driver's seat, praising through her tears. This rhythm—lament giving way to praise—is a cornerstone of African American spirituality. In therapy, we call it emotional regulation; in the Spirit, it is worship that heals.

By Saturday, she sat across from her therapist, feeling lighter but still raw. Together they looked at a feelings wheel, a chart mapping emotions from broad categories to something more precise, sharper. Like her true feelings were finally seen. For the first time, she realized her anger was often covering feelings of being "disrespected," "overwhelmed," and "lonely." Naming those feelings mattered. It turned her shame into language she could pray through: "Lord, meet me in my loneliness. Steady me when I feel overwhelmed." Therapy had given her words; faith helped her offer those words to God.

Resilience, for Tiana, wasn't one grand turning point. It was these daily choices: to whisper trust when anxiety rose, to let scripture anchor her mornings, to show up for community, to cry and praise in the same breath, to let therapy expand her language

189

and prayer deepen her healing. These choices built buffers where trauma had stripped them away. They didn't erase her struggles, but they kept her from being crushed under their weight.

And they can do the same for you.

So let me ask you: what would it look like if you stepped into Tiana's shoes this week?

Maybe it begins with a whisper when the stress tightens your chest: "Lord, I can't carry this alone." Maybe it's writing down one verse on a sticky note and putting it where your eyes will land every morning. Maybe it's saying yes to that Bible study, small group, or prayer call you've been avoiding because you didn't want to feel exposed. Maybe it's giving yourself permission to cry to a gospel song on your commute, letting lament flow and then lifting your voice in praise. Or maybe it's finally naming your feelings out loud—whether in therapy, in prayer, or in your journal—so you don't keep swallowing them whole.

Resilience doesn't come all at once, and it doesn't mean you'll never feel pressed again. It means that when the weight presses in, you will not be crushed—because Christ is your buffer, and your community is your witness. Like Tiana, you can begin again, one small practice at a time.

Reflection and Invitation

Before moving on, take a moment to pause. This chapter has explored what it means to live resiliently—not by our own strength, but through the sustaining presence of Christ and the support of His people. Resilience isn't about pretending life hasn't pressed us down. It's about testifying that in the pressing, we were not crushed.

I want to invite you to reflect on your own journey:

- What does resilience mean to you in this season of your life?
- Can you name a moment when you felt "pressed, but not crushed"?
- How has Christ served as your buffer in times of trial?

These questions are not about getting the "right" answer—they are about making space for honesty. Resilience is born in the places where we admit we are fragile and yet still choose to hope.

Journaling Exercise: Your Resilience Testimony

Take some time to write your own resilience testimony. Begin by naming a past struggle—something that felt overwhelming, something you thought might undo you. Then trace how you endured. Where did God meet you? Who or what served as your buffer? How did you carry both the death and the life of Jesus in that season?

You may be surprised by what comes to the surface. Sometimes, looking back, we realize we were stronger than we knew—not because of willpower, but because Christ was alive within us, renewing us day by day.

If you feel comfortable, you may even want to share your resilience testimony with someone you trust—in your small group, in your church community, or with a close friend. Testimonies don't just encourage others; they remind us of what God has already done and what He is still able to do.

Resilience is not a solo achievement. It is the story of Christ's life showing up in ours, again and again. As you write, remember: your fragility does not disqualify you. You are a jar of clay, but within you is treasure. And that treasure is enough to carry you through.

Lord Jesus,

You see the places where I feel pressed and overwhelmed.

Thank You that I am not crushed, not abandoned, not destroyed—because You are with me.

Teach me to trust You when life feels too heavy to bear.

Help me to name my emotions with honesty, to pray with both lament and praise, and to lean into the community You've given me for strength.

Remind me that my fragility is not failure—for in these jars of clay, Your treasure shines through.

Renew me day by day, and let my life be a testimony of Your sustaining power.

Amen.

CHAPTER 10

Forgiveness

I need to be honest with you.

I didn't want to write this chapter either.

When I sat down to write this book, I never planned to include a section on forgiveness. My focus was resilience and healing. But every time I tried to move forward, or thought the manuscript was complete, I felt in my spirit that something was missing. It was like I was trying to close a door while something inside kept pounding to get out. That "something" was forgiveness. I realized that if I ignored it, the story of healing would remain incomplete. God cannot place the healing we long for into hands that are still clenched with unforgiveness.

The truth is, forgiveness has always been complicated for our community. How many times have we been told to "just forgive" while the harm kept coming? How many pulpits have rushed us past our anger, past our grief, into a shallow grace that left us feeling silenced? We've been told to forgive slavery. To forgive Jim Crow. To forgive police brutality. To forgive broken families. To forgive absent fathers. To forgive mothers who couldn't give what they never had.

And in our personal lives, the same pattern repeats. We've been told to forgive betrayal, abuse, abandonment, disrespect—all without acknowledgment of the weight we carry.

As I write, I think of you and the way you hold it all together. Maybe you're raising kids on your own, clocking in at work even when your heart feels heavy. Maybe you've smiled through a family gathering where the very people who hurt you sat across the table, and you kept quiet because "keeping the peace" felt safer than naming the truth. Maybe you've prayed for God to take away the bitterness, but the memories still live in your body like fire in your chest. You love the Lord, but you also feel the weight of unhealed wounds.

And when people talk about forgiveness, it almost feels like they're asking you to let your abuser, your oppressor, your betrayer off the hook.

But here's the thing: that's not the forgiveness I'm talking about.

Forgiveness doesn't mean pretending it didn't hurt. It doesn't mean rushing back into a relationship with someone who hasn't changed. It doesn't mean excusing, minimizing, or erasing the truth. Forgiveness is invitation, not requirement; if you're unsafe, your first call is safety.

The forgiveness I want to talk about here is different. It's the kind that makes you free.

Because the secret no one tells you is this: when we hold on to unforgiveness, we think we're punishing the other person, but in reality, we're the ones locked up. Our bodies stay tight with tension. Our nervous system keeps replaying the injury. Our minds rehearse the same story like a broken record. Clinically, unforgiveness shows up as anxiety, depression, sleepless nights, even high blood pressure. Spiritually, it feels like walking around with chains around your neck.

Sis, I don't want you living with a jailer. I don't want you waking up every morning still giving the person who hurt you more power than they deserve. Forgiveness is not about helping them—it's about setting you free.

Here's the part I need you to hear: you don't forgive out of your own strength. None of us can. We forgive because we are connected to a love bigger than us. The love of Christ is limitless, and that love is our refuge. When God says, "Vengeance is mine; I will repay" (Romans 12:19), He isn't letting people off the hook—He's promising that He sees, He knows, and He will handle it. That means you don't have to carry the bitterness anymore.

Forgiveness does not erase the need for accountability. It can coexist with accountability, restitution, and legal action. Throughout Scripture, repentance is paired with repair—Zacchaeus, for example, confessed his wrongs and made restitution (Luke 19:8). In the same way, naming harm and requiring repair is part of biblical justice. Forgiveness frees your heart, but it does not cancel the need for truth-telling and change.

Forgiveness is about release. It means you stop being your own jailer. It means you step out of the prison cell of anger and into the wide-open air of freedom.

Does it happen overnight? No. Sometimes forgiveness comes in layers. Sometimes you'll forgive today and feel the anger rise up again tomorrow. That's okay. Forgiveness is not a one-time act; it's a process of loosening the chain, one link at a time, until you can breathe again.

Researchers have even mapped forgiveness as a process with stages, not a single moment. Models like REACH or Enright's phases describe steps—naming the hurt, choosing to release, finding meaning, and sometimes circling back again. You don't have to follow a script, but it can help to know there's a path, with room for setbacks and returns along the way.

That's why we have to talk about it here. Because without forgiveness, healing will always feel unfinished. And I want you whole.

What Forgiveness Is—and Is Not

Before we can talk about how to forgive, we need to clear away the lies you've been told about forgiveness. Because if you carry the wrong definition, you'll feel stuck, guilty, or even unsafe when the word comes up.

Forgiveness is not forgetting

Some people will tell you, "Just let it go, just move on." But forgetting is not the same thing as forgiving. Forgetting dishonors your pain. Forgetting tries to erase something that really happened, as if your heart and body can be tricked into silence.

Even God doesn't ask us to forget. Over and over in Scripture, God tells His people to remember. Remember the slavery in Egypt. Remember the covenant. Remember the works of His hand. Memory is not the enemy—memory is the place where healing begins. The psalmist cried out, "How long, O Lord?" (Psalm 13:1). That cry is holy. It means we name the wound before we move toward hope.

Forgiveness is not reconciliation

Reconciliation is beautiful when it happens, but it requires two people. It requires repentance, accountability, and safety. Forgiveness, on the other hand, is between you and God. You can forgive someone fully in your heart and still set boundaries that protect your peace. In fact, boundaries are often the most faithful way to honor the healing God is doing in you.

Maybe you've been told, "If you really forgave, you'd let them back in." But that's pressure, not Scripture. Even Jesus didn't entrust Himself to everyone (John 2:24). Forgiveness doesn't require you to return to harm.

Forgiveness is not approval

You don't forgive because you agree with what was done. You don't forgive because you've decided it wasn't that bad. Forgiveness doesn't shrink the wound. It names it for what it was—and then refuses to let that act be the headline of your story.

Think of it this way: forgiveness does not minimize the wound, but it does minimize the wound's power to define you.

Forgiveness is not weakness

Sis, don't let anyone tell you that forgiveness makes you soft or naïve. Forgiveness takes strength that only God can provide. It takes courage to lay down anger when it has felt like your only protection. It takes faith to trust God with justice you may never see in your lifetime.

Forgiveness is fierce. Forgiveness is brave. Forgiveness is strength dressed in grace.

So then, what is forgiveness?

Forgiveness is a conscious act of release. It is looking at the wound with honesty, naming it for what it is, and then deciding: This will not control me anymore.

Clinically, we know that unforgiveness keeps your nervous system stuck in overdrive. Your brain replays the betrayal as if it's still happening. Your body carries the tension. Your sleep gets disrupted. Your energy drains. But when you begin to forgive, your body finally finds space to rest. Your heart rate slows. Your mind stops rehearsing the story on repeat. Joy has room to breathe again.

Spiritually, forgiveness is entrusting justice to God. It's saying, "Lord, I hand this over to You because I believe You are my defender." It's not pretending the hurt didn't matter—it's declaring that God's justice and love matter more than your anger.

And forgiveness is freedom. Freedom to live untethered. Freedom to stop rehearsing the old pain. Freedom to reclaim your energy and pour it into your children, your calling, your healing, your joy. Freedom to breathe fully again.

So let me ask you, gently:

- What stories are you still carrying in your chest?
- Who is still living rent-free in your spirit because you haven't let them go?
- What would open up in your life if you chose release—even before reconciliation?

Forgiveness is not about letting them win. It's about letting God's love win in you.

The Chains of Unforgiveness

Let me be real with you: unforgiveness is heavy.

At first, it can feel like protection. You tell yourself, "I'll never let them get away with what they did. I'll hold on to this anger—it's the only thing keeping me strong." And that makes sense. Anger can feel powerful. Bitterness can feel like armor. But here's the hard truth: while you're holding on to that pain, that pain is holding on to you. Don't get me wrong though, Anger itself is not sin—it is data. It is a protector; forgiveness doesn't require you to stop feeling, it changes who holds the steering wheel. In Scripture, righteous anger often served as protest and protection; the psalms of lament even cry out for justice with fierce honesty. Anger can be a boundary signal, showing us where something sacred has been violated. The danger comes only when anger festers into bitterness that consumes us.

Unforgiveness is like carrying around chains. You can still move, but everything feels slower, heavier. Even when you laugh, the chains rattle. Even when you work, the weight drags behind you.

Your Body Keeps the Score

Clinically, we know unforgiveness keeps your nervous system stuck in survival mode. Maybe you've noticed it: the tightness in your shoulders, the pit in your stomach, the restless nights when your thoughts won't stop racing. It's your body saying, "We're still in danger."

When bitterness builds, cortisol—the body's stress hormone—stays high. Your heart beats faster. Your immune system weakens. Sleep escapes you. Joy feels like a stranger.

It Steals Your Presence

Unforgiveness shows up emotionally, too. Have you ever snapped at your children, not because of what they did, but because of all the weight you're carrying inside? Have you been in worship, hands lifted, but felt your mind drifting back to the one who hurt you, unable to fully trust God because bitterness had taken center stage? That's the chain at work. It hijacks your peace. It robs you of being fully here.

Spiritually, It Keeps You Bound

And spiritually, those chains tether you to the very person you want freedom from. As Archbishop Desmond Tutu teaches, "Without forgiveness, we remain tethered to the person who harmed us. We are bound with chains of bitterness, tied together, trapped. Until we can forgive, that person will hold the keys to our happiness; that person will be our jailor."

Think about that for a moment: the one who hurt you still holding the keys to your peace. That's not fair. That's not freedom.

Sis, God never meant for you to live with a jailer. Jesus declared that He came to "set the captives free" (Luke 4:18). That includes you. Forgiveness is the way you take the keys back. Forgiveness breaks the lock, loosens the chain, and opens the door so you can walk out into the wholeness God designed for you.

The Risk and the Reward

I know—it feels risky to even imagine forgiving. It feels like letting go means they "got away with it." But forgiveness doesn't mean they escape accountability. It means you refuse to let them steal one more day of your life.

When you forgive, you declare:

- "You don't get to control my joy."
- "You don't get to keep me in prison."
- "God has the keys now, and I'm walking free."

Forgiveness in your heart does not mean staying silent in the face of injustice. You can forgive and still pursue justice through the courts, through restorative processes, or by challenging broken systems. Release frees you from bondage; it does not cancel your right to seek repair.

Take, for example, a woman who forgives her abusive partner in her heart. That forgiveness frees her from carrying the poison of rage every day—but it does not mean she stays silent or remains in danger. She still pursues a restraining order. She still testifies in court. She still holds him accountable through the justice system. Her forgiveness is about release; her pursuit of justice is about protection and repair. The two can exist side by side.

Forgiveness as Self-Interest and Liberation

Here's something most of us were never taught growing up: forgiveness is one of the most powerful acts of self-interest you will ever choose.

That may sound strange at first. We're used to thinking of forgiveness as something we do "for them"—for the person who hurt us, for the family who betrayed us, for the oppressor who never repented. But that's not the kind of forgiveness I'm talking about.

When you forgive, you are not saying, "What you did was okay." You are saying, "What you did will no longer control me." That shift changes everything.

Clinically Speaking

Research confirms what our spirits already know: forgiveness heals.

- People who practice forgiveness experience lower blood pressure, stronger immune systems, and better heart health.
- Forgiveness reduces cortisol, the stress hormone that floods your body when you're carrying bitterness.
- It helps you sleep better. It eases anxiety and depression.
- It even extends life expectancy.

Although research does show forgiveness can lower stress hormones, strengthen immunity, and even support longer life. Trauma severity, timing, and safety all shape how the body responds. Forgiveness is not a one-size-fits-all cure, yet it can open space for healing when the conditions are right. Think about that: forgiving someone who hurt you could potentially add years to your life. That's how much the body suffers under the weight of unforgiveness.

Bitterness doesn't just poison relationships. It poisons your cells. It clogs your joy, drains your energy, and keeps you locked in survival mode. Forgiveness becomes a kind of medicine. Every time you release a piece of bitterness, your nervous system gets a chance to rest, your breath deepens, and your body remembers peace.

It's also important to say: symptoms like nightmares, hyperarousal, or depression may persist even after deep and genuine forgiveness. If symptoms persist, that's not a failure of forgiveness—seek trauma-informed care. Sometimes trauma lives on in the nervous system, and healing may require therapy, body-based work, or medical support alongside forgiveness. Your worth and faith are not measured by symptom relief alone.

Spiritually Speaking
But forgiveness isn't just healthy — it's holy.

When you forgive, you step into the freedom Christ already won for you. You're saying: "I trust God to handle the justice, and I refuse to carry this weight another day."

The apostle Paul reminded the Romans: "Do not take revenge, my dear friends, but leave room for God's wrath. For it is written: 'It is mine to avenge; I will repay,' says the Lord" (Romans 12:19).

Sis, forgiveness doesn't mean God ignores what was done to you. Quite the opposite. It means you are no longer dragging yourself into the courtroom of your mind every single day, trying to be judge, jury, and executioner. Forgiveness means you hand the case to the only righteous Judge — and then you walk free.

The Liberation Shift

When you forgive, you reclaim your energy. Instead of pouring your strength into rehearsing old pain, you redirect it toward your healing, your children, your calling, your joy.

Forgiveness means declaring:

- "I will not let you define me."
- "I will not let bitterness poison my spirit."
- "I choose freedom over chains."

Forgiveness is not weakness — it is courage. It is choosing to be your own liberator. It is standing tall and saying, "My life, my peace, my joy are too valuable to stay trapped in someone else's hands."

The Role of Love in Forgiveness

Sis, let's be real: left to our own strength, forgiveness is impossible. Some wounds cut so deep they don't just bruise the skin — they bruise the soul. When you've been betrayed, abandoned, abused, or oppressed, you can't just will yourself into forgiveness.

That's why forgiveness has to be rooted in something larger than us. And that something is love. Not just any love — limitless love.

Human Love Has Limits

Here's the truth: human love runs out.

- Maybe you told yourself you forgave, but then the memory came back and your chest tightened all over again.
- Maybe you tried to move on, but every time you saw their face, the anger rose up like it just happened yesterday.
- Maybe you prayed for strength, but deep down, you still felt the grudge burning in your chest.

That's not failure — that's human. Our love has limits.

God's Love Does Not

But God's love? His love is endless. It never wears out, never dries up, never walks away. Scripture tells us: "The steadfast love of the Lord never ceases; His mercies never come to an end; they are new every morning" (Lamentations 3:22–23).

That means every day you wake up with access to a fresh supply of love — enough to carry you, enough to heal you, and yes, enough to help you forgive.

Forgiveness isn't about digging deeper into your own empty well. It's about drawing from God's well, where the water never runs dry.

Christ's Example

Think about Jesus on the cross. Beaten, betrayed, humiliated — and still He prayed, "Father, forgive them, for they know not what they do" (Luke 23:34). That wasn't human strength. That was divine love pouring through Him.

And the same Spirit that gave Jesus strength to forgive is alive in you. That same love flows through you, even when you feel empty.

Love as Refuge

This is what makes forgiveness safe: you don't have to trade hurt for approval. You don't have to let someone back into your life just to prove you forgave them. You don't even have to feel like forgiving before you begin the process.

All you need is to take refuge in the love of Christ — the kind of love that whispers:

- "I see your pain, and I still call you mine."
- "You don't have to carry bitterness — let Me carry you."
- "Justice belongs to Me. You are free."

Sis, forgiveness becomes possible because love makes it possible. Love defends you. Love heals you. Love empowers you to do what your own strength cannot.

Forgiveness is not about letting them win — it's about letting God's love win in you.

Understanding, Perspective-Taking, and Boundaries

Now, let me be clear: forgiveness does not mean you excuse what happened. It doesn't mean you rewrite the story to make it look prettier. The wound is still the wound. The truth is still the truth.

But sometimes, as healing unfolds, part of forgiveness involves perspective-taking—not to justify the harm, but to help release the weight it left behind.

Perspective-Taking Can Loosen the Grip

Maybe you had a parent who was emotionally absent. For years, you carried that absence like proof that you were unworthy of love. But over time, you began to see differently: your parent wasn't absent because you weren't lovable—they were absent because they were broken, carrying wounds they never healed.

Does that excuse the neglect? Absolutely not. But does it help you see that their failure was about their pain, not your worth? Yes. And that shift loosens the grip of bitterness.

Clinically, this is what we call reframing. The story is the same, but the meaning changes. Your nervous system relaxes when it realizes, "This was not my fault. I am not defined by their brokenness."

Perspective-taking can sometimes soften our grip on resentment—but hear me clearly: empathy is never a prerequisite for safety or forgiveness. If you've survived deep harm or abuse, you are not required to imagine the other person's viewpoint as part of your healing. Empathy is an optional, later-stage practice some may choose once safety and boundaries are firmly in place.

Boundaries Protect Healing

But don't get it twisted: perspective is not permission. You can understand someone's story and still choose not to let them harm you again.

Forgiveness says, "I release you from the debt."

Boundaries say, "But I will not allow you to keep withdrawing from my account."

Sis, boundaries are not un-Christian; they are holy wisdom. Even Jesus set boundaries. He often withdrew from the crowds to pray. He didn't entrust Himself to everyone (John 2:24). If our Savior guarded His peace, how much more should we?

So yes, you can forgive your father for leaving, but still choose not to let him disrupt the peace of your home. You can forgive a friend who betrayed your trust, but still decide not to open your heart to them again. You can forgive a church or community that wounded you, but still worship in a space where your spirit feels safe.

Love and Wisdom Walk Together

The Apostle Paul prayed this over the Philippians: "That your love may abound more and more in knowledge and depth of insight, so that you may be able to discern what is best" (Philippians 1:9–10). That's forgiveness with wisdom.

Love doesn't mean naivety. Forgiveness doesn't mean recklessness. Love plus wisdom means freedom plus protection.

Forgiveness plus understanding helps release you from bitterness.

Forgiveness plus boundaries helps protect your healing.

Together, they create space for you to live free—unbound, wise, and safe.

Forgiveness Without Reconciliation

This may be the hardest truth to face: forgiveness and reconciliation are not the same thing.

Reconciliation is beautiful when it happens, but it requires two willing hearts. It requires repentance, accountability, safety, and trust being rebuilt over time. Forgiveness, on the other hand, is something you can choose today, with or without the other person's participation.

When Reconciliation Isn't Possible

Maybe the person who hurt you has passed away. The apology you longed for will never come.

Maybe they're still alive but unrepentant—justifying their actions, making excuses, or refusing to change.

Maybe you know deep down that letting them back into your life would only open the door for more harm.

In those cases, reconciliation may never come. And that's okay. Forgiveness is still possible.

Releasing Without Returning

Forgiveness does not require you to return to the scene of the crime.

Forgiveness does not demand that you invite the same pain back into your life.

You can forgive your father who never showed up, even if he never calls to apologize.

You can forgive the family member who gossiped about you, even if you never confide in them again.

You can forgive the ex who mistreated you, even if you never see them again.

Forgiveness says: "I release you, but I release myself too. You no longer get to hold my peace hostage."

Boundaries Are Holy

In some church spaces, people have been told, "If you really forgave them, you'd reconcile." But that's not Scripture—that's pressure. Forgiveness must never be demanded or extracted—especially not by the very systems or people who caused harm. Family, churches, or workplaces may have tried to pressure you into silence under the banner of forgiveness. True forgiveness can only be chosen freely, in your own timing. And safety always comes first: if reconciliation is even considered, it must be preceded by clear safety planning and accountability.

Even God does not force reconciliation without repentance. He offers forgiveness freely, but He calls it reconciliation only when we repent and turn toward Him. If even God draws that distinction, why wouldn't we?

Boundaries are not a lack of forgiveness—they are proof of wisdom. They say, "I can let go of bitterness without letting you back into the same place of access."

Historical and Personal Layers

This truth matters not just personally, but collectively. As Black people, we can forgive the colonizers and enslavers for what was done to our ancestors, but that doesn't mean we reconcile with the systems that still cause harm. Forgiveness lets us walk in freedom. Reconciliation requires justice.

And in our personal lives, the same is true. Forgiveness is unilateral—you can do it in prayer, in therapy, in the quiet of your own heart. Reconciliation is mutual—and sometimes it's just not safe.

Freedom Without Permission

So hear me clearly, sis: your forgiveness is still real, still valid, still holy, even if reconciliation never happens. You don't need the offender's permission to forgive. You don't need their acknowledgment to be free.

Forgiveness is between you and God. It is your liberation.

Practical Pathways to Forgiveness

Sis, forgiveness isn't just something we talk about. These exercises are designed to help you walk the path little by little. Take your time. There's no rush. Healing is holy work, and it unfolds at your pace.

Here is a map you can return to when the road to forgiveness feels unclear.

211

- Name the hurt – Acknowledge what happened and how it wounded you. No minimizing. No sugarcoating.

- Feel the weight – Allow the anger, grief, and lament to be seen. These emotions are data, not sin.

- Choose release – Decide, in your own timing, to loosen resentment's grip. This may happen in layers.

- Seek meaning – Look for how God can bring growth, strength, or clarity out of pain—without excusing the harm.

- Repeat as needed – Forgiveness isn't linear. You may revisit these steps many times, each bringing a little more freedom.

1. Journaling Letters (Never Sent)

Purpose: To release words and emotions that have been locked inside.

If you carry deep or traumatic wounds, know that writing about them can sometimes stir up intense emotions. That doesn't mean you're doing it wrong, it just means your body is remembering. To care for yourself, set a time limit (10–15 minutes), have a grounding practice ready (deep breaths, feeling your feet on the floor), and plan a gentle ritual afterward like making tea, taking a short walk, or calling a trusted friend. Forgiveness work should never leave you feeling unsafe or alone.

Exercise:

Write a letter that begins:

"This is what you did to me… This is how it made me feel… This is what I carried because of it…"

Then shift your focus:

"Today I release you. You no longer get to hold my peace hostage. I choose to forgive, and I take my freedom back."

You do not have to send this letter. The power is in writing it.

Reflection Prompt:

After writing, ask yourself:

- What emotions rose up in me?

- Where in my body did I feel tension as I wrote?

- What feels lighter now?

2. Somatic Release Practice

Purpose: To release unforgiveness not just from the mind, but from the body.

If you tend to 'check out' or feel far away when slowing down to breathe, try orienting first with the 5-4-3-2-1 grounding exercise: notice 5 things you can see, 4 things you can touch, 3 things you can hear, 2 things you can smell, and 1 thing you can taste. Once your body feels more present, then move into the breath count. This helps anchor you before deeper release.

Exercise:

- Place your hand over your heart. Inhale deeply for 4 counts, exhale slowly for 6.

- On each exhale, whisper: "I choose freedom."

- Repeat for 3–5 minutes.

Reflection Prompt:

Write down:

- What did I notice in my body before and after this practice?

- Did my breath feel different?

- Did I sense God's presence as I released?

3. Narrative Reframing

Purpose: To retell the story with new meaning, moving from shame to truth.

Reframing is powerful, but it should only be done when you feel safe and supported. It is never about minimizing abuse or excusing sin. The goal is not to rewrite the harm, but to reclaim your story on your own terms.

Exercise:

- Write down a painful belief connected to unforgiveness (e.g., "I was abandoned, so I must be unworthy.").

- Now reframe it: "They abandoned me because of their brokenness, not my worth. God has never abandoned me."

- What new truth is God inviting me to claim about myself?

- How does this reframe shift my perspective?

4. Prayer and Lament

Purpose: To bring your pain honestly before God.

Exercise:

- Write a prayer of lament that begins: "Lord, this hurt me deeply. I feel…"

- Be raw, unfiltered, unpolished.

- Then close with: "And still, I release this to You. Help me forgive, even when my heart resists."

- Consider using prayer postures: kneeling, lifting hands, or lying prostrate as a way of symbolically laying down the burden before God.

Reflection Prompt:
What was it like to be this honest with God?
Did I sense Him receiving my pain?

5. Scripture Meditation

Purpose: To anchor forgiveness in God's promises.

Exercise:

- Choose one Scripture (Romans 12:19, Exodus 14:14, or 1 Peter 5:7).

- Write it on a sticky note or index card.

- Speak it aloud each morning for one week.

Reflection Prompt:
- How did speaking God's Word daily shift my thoughts or emotions?
- Did it change how I felt toward the person I'm forgiving?

6. Communal Support

Purpose: To remember you don't have to do this alone.

Note: Not everyone is equipped to walk with you through deep wounds. Choose helpers who are trauma-informed—like a licensed therapist, a trained prayer minister, or a mentor who understands boundaries. Well-meaning but unskilled friends can sometimes re-open wounds rather than help them heal.

Exercise:
- Identify one safe person (friend, mentor, therapist, or prayer partner) who can walk with you in this journey.
- Share with them: "I'm working on releasing bitterness. Will you walk with me?"

Reflection Prompt:
- Who can I lean on in this process?
- What would it feel like to not carry this burden by myself?

Forgiving Ourselves: When the Person You Must Forgive Is You

Sometimes, the hardest person to forgive is not the one who hurt us—it's ourselves.

Many of us carry silent shame for the ways we responded when we were under pressure: for staying in harmful situations, for freezing when we wanted to run, for not "seeing it sooner," or for keeping quiet to keep the peace. These choices can replay in our minds like accusations: Why didn't I do more? Why didn't I fight back? Why didn't I leave?

From a trauma perspective, those responses—freeze, fawn, comply—were not moral failures. They were survival instincts. God designed our nervous systems to protect us in overwhelming circumstances. The body chooses the safest option it can access in the moment, whether that's shutting down, appeasing, or holding still until the danger passes. When you look back and judge yourself, you're often judging a younger version of you who had fewer resources and was simply trying to live through the day.

Scripture reminds us that God "knows our frame; He remembers that we are dust" (Psalm 103:14). He is not surprised by our fragility. There is "no condemnation for those who are in Christ Jesus" (Romans 8:1), and that includes condemnation we heap on ourselves. If the Lord Himself chooses mercy, who are we to deny it to ourselves?

Self-forgiveness is not about excusing sin or pretending mistakes don't matter. It's about releasing ourselves from shame so that we can walk in freedom. Think about Peter, who denied Jesus three times. His grief was real, but when Christ restored him by the sea, the invitation was not to stay trapped in regret—it was to feed the sheep, to move forward in love and purpose. God's grace didn't erase Peter's history; it redeemed it.

The same can be true for us. Self-forgiveness means telling yourself the truth: I did the best I could with what I had at the time. I am not defined by my trauma responses. I am not bound to shame forever. When you forgive yourself, you unclench the fist you've been holding against your own chest. You open your hands to receive God's mercy, already extended toward you.

A Practice for You: A Letter of Compassion

Take a moment to write a letter to yourself—maybe to the age or season when you felt most ashamed. Begin by naming what you went through: "You were scared. You were overwhelmed. You were doing what you could to survive." Then speak words of compassion: "I don't blame you. You didn't fail. You did what you needed to do, and I release you from the guilt you've carried." Close the letter with a blessing: "I forgive you. I love you. I choose to let you be free."

If writing feels too intense, you can speak these words aloud in front of a mirror, or imagine your younger self sitting across from you and offer them the grace you wish you had received back then.

Reflection Questions

- What parts of your story feel heavy with shame?

- Can you name a survival response (freeze, fawn, comply) you once judged as failure, but now recognize as protection?

- How might God be inviting you to extend grace to yourself in that area?

A Gentle Reminder

Forgiving yourself is not a one-time event. Just like forgiving others, it often happens in layers. You may feel free today and feel shame creep back in tomorrow. That doesn't mean you've failed. It means you are human. Keep practicing. Each time you offer yourself mercy, you loosen shame's grip a little more.

And remember: releasing yourself from shame doesn't erase the need for healing support. For some, trauma work with a therapist or safe community is an essential companion to this journey. Self-forgiveness creates the space for deeper healing to take root.

Closing Note: Forgiveness is not a quick fix. It's a rhythm, not a one-time event. Some days you may feel free, and other days the chain may tug again. That doesn't mean you've failed — it means you're human. Keep practicing. Every time you choose release, you loosen bitterness's grip and step closer to freedom.

Forgiveness work can be sealed through ritual—something embodied and concrete that helps your soul recognize release. In our traditions, that might mean burning the unsent letter and watching the smoke rise like prayer. It might mean anointing yourself with oil as a sign of consecration and new beginning. Some choose to lay a stone on the ground as a marker, or visit a graveside and speak words of release when the person has passed. These embodied acts are not magic; they are reminders that what God has begun in your spirit is real and lasting.

Lord,

You see the places in my heart that are still tender, still aching, still bound by what was done to me. You know the tears I've cried in secret, the anger I've carried, the ways bitterness has weighed me down.

I confess that forgiveness feels hard—sometimes it feels impossible. But I also know You never created me to live chained to the ones who hurt me. You created me for freedom.

So today, I make a choice—not because I feel ready, but because I trust You. I choose to forgive. I release this person into Your hands. I release the wound, the memory, the anger, and the bitterness. I give them to You, Lord, because You are just, You are loving, and You are my defender.

You promised that vengeance belongs to You. You promised that You will repay. That means I don't have to carry the weight of justice on my shoulders. I don't have to be my own judge. I trust You to handle what I cannot.

Fill me with Your love—the kind of love that has no limits. Cover the cracks in my heart with Your healing presence. Teach me how to walk in freedom, to guard my peace with wisdom, and to love myself enough to let go.

And when the hurt rises again tomorrow, remind me to come back here, to this place of release. Keep teaching me to forgive, little by little, until my soul is light again.

Thank You for carrying what I can't. Thank You for being my refuge, my healer, and my vindicator.

In Jesus' name,

Amen.

CHAPTER 11

The Process of Healing

Taking a Deep Breath: Entering the Work of Healing

After wrestling with what forgiveness means—and what it does not mean—we now arrive at the threshold of healing. Forgiveness loosens the chains that keep us bound to the one who harmed us, but healing is what allows us to walk forward with strength, dignity, and hope.

Healing is not a single event, and it is certainly not a straight line. It is not a mountain to be conquered in one heroic climb. Healing is more like a long walk: sometimes the path is smooth and open, other times it is steep and uneven. There will be moments when you feel energized and light, and moments when you feel weary and wonder if the effort is worth it. All of this is part of the process.

In this chapter, we'll walk alongside Serena from the introduction once again. When we first met her, she sat on the edge of her bed, heart pounding as she turned her phone face down. She longed to be loved, but fear kept whispering, "They'll leave eventually." Her past taught her to doubt joy, to retreat into silence, to confuse distance with safety.

But Serena is still here. She hasn't given up. She wants something more than the ache of mistrust and the illusion of safety. Like so many of us, she is realizing that if she is going to step into new life, she will have to begin the slow, steady work of healing—not just forgiving, not just surviving, but becoming whole.

So before we take another step, take a deep breath. Let your body know that you are safe enough to do this work. Let your spirit remember that you were made for wholeness. And let your mind rest in the truth that while the path of healing is long, it is possible—and you are already on your way.

Understanding How Change Works

Healing and change are not mysteries. They may feel overwhelming at first, but there is a rhythm to how people grow. Once you recognize that rhythm, you can better understand where you are in the process and what it will take to keep going.

The Mechanics of Change

Change involves more than one decision. It asks us to shift behaviors, thought patterns, and emotional responses together. Psychologists Prochaska and DiClemente describe this as a series of stages:

- **Pre-contemplation** – You don't think change is necessary. Life feels heavy, but you may still say, "This is just who I am."
- **Contemplation** – You begin to wonder, What if things could be different?
- **Preparation** – You start planning small steps, like looking for a therapist or setting healthier boundaries.
- **Action** – You practice new behaviors, even though they feel uncomfortable.
- **Maintenance** – You create routines that help you stay consistent.

- **Relapse** – You slip back into old habits, which isn't failure—it's part of the process.

Each stage is important, and none of them make you a failure. In therapy we often use the word 'relapse,' but here I prefer to think of it as a 'recycle' or a 'flare-up.' Healing is cyclical, not linear. A flare-up isn't failure—it's feedback. It shows us where we need a little more support, a gentler pace, or one more tiny adjustment on the journey. The stages simply describe where you are on the journey. Healing requires not just doing differently but also thinking differently. A new behavior without a new mindset won't hold for long.

Serena's Journey Through Change

Serena didn't always believe she needed to change. After her last relationship unraveled, she sat with the ache and told herself the same story she had rehearsed for years: This is just who I am. I love too hard. I'm too much. I'll always push people away. Life felt heavy, but in her mind, her patterns were woven into her very personality. She couldn't imagine herself any other way.

And yet, one quiet evening, something shifted. Sitting cross-legged on her bed, the glow of her phone lighting up the room, she wondered, What if I don't have to keep living like this? The question startled her. She thought of women in her church who seemed to carry both love and strength, who didn't crumble at the first sign of distance. For the first time, Serena let herself imagine a different possibility: Maybe it could be different for me too.

That thought lingered long enough for her to take a step. The following week, she opened her laptop and began searching for therapists. Her hands trembled as she typed, but she pressed forward. She told a close friend, "I think I need help." It wasn't a grand plan—it was small, hesitant, but it was preparation. She was no longer only dreaming of change; she was positioning herself to step into it.

The real test came with action. Serena booked her first therapy session, her heart pounding as she clicked "confirm." Sitting across from the therapist, she said out loud words she had never admitted before: "I don't trust people to stay." It felt both terrifying and freeing. Later that week, when she felt the urge to send three anxious texts in a row, she practiced pausing, breathing, and writing her feelings in a journal instead. It felt awkward, unnatural, like trying on shoes that didn't quite fit. But it was action all the same.

With time, those awkward steps began to form a rhythm. Serena created routines that supported her growth: journaling before reacting, practicing deep breathing when fear tightened her chest, leaning on her support group when doubt crept in. These small practices built a structure she could return to. Slowly, her new way of being became more familiar.

Still, there were nights when old habits resurfaced. An unanswered text could still send her spiraling, and sometimes she pressed "send" on messages she later regretted. At first, she felt crushed by shame, convinced she had undone all her progress. But therapy taught her that relapse wasn't the end of change, it was part of it. Each time she stumbled, she noticed she could find her footing again more quickly. Her setbacks became teachers, showing her where her wounds still needed tending and reminding her she had tools to return to.

Serena's story reminds us that healing is not a straight climb but a cycle: forward, back, forward again. Each step, even a shaky one, is part of the process.

Where People Get Stuck

One of the greatest challenges is that we often confuse survival adaptations with personality traits. We say things like:

- "I'm just not good with people."
- "I'll always have a temper."
- "That's just how I am."

But many of these so-called traits are actually patterns we picked up to survive unsafe environments. Silence may have been necessary as a child. Distrust may have kept us from being hurt again. But what once protected us now holds us back.

Serena wrestled with this herself. She had grown up believing her mistrust was part of her personality. "I'm just difficult to love," she often told herself after relationships fell apart. But in truth, her suspicion and hypervigilance were not personality flaws, they were survival skills she had learned in a childhood where stability was fragile and love had to be earned. What once shielded her heart was now a wall shutting love out.

Another stumbling block is expecting external change to fix internal wounds. We lose weight, but in our minds we are still carrying the old body. We get the new job, but we still feel unworthy. We enter a new relationship, but the fear of abandonment poisons it from the start.

Serena knew that cycle too. When she finally started dating someone kind and patient, she expected her fear to vanish. But instead of resting in his presence, she braced for the moment he would leave. Even though the external situation had changed, her inner story had not. The real work wasn't just about finding a healthy partner—it was about becoming the kind of woman who believed she was worthy of being loved.

The Relationship Between Identity and Healing

Change is always tied to identity. We attract not only what we want, but who we believe we are. The first time I heard this, I bristled. It felt like someone was telling me I was the reason for my pain, that my wounds were proof I hadn't believed the right things about myself. But that's not what this means. It isn't about blame, it's about alignment. If deep down I believe I am unworthy, I will shrink from opportunities that require confidence. If I believe everyone leaves, I will push away someone who actually wants to stay. If I believe my voice doesn't matter, I will never use it, even when God is calling me to speak. Healing requires more than new behaviors. It requires a new way of seeing ourselves. It requires us to see ourselves the way God already sees us. Without that shift, we may find ourselves sabotaging the very blessings we've prayed for.

Serena had to confront this after the end of her previous relationship. She prayed earnestly for a godly, emotionally healthy spouse. Deep down, she longed for a partner who would love her without games or manipulation. But at the same time, she was so entrenched in hyper-independence—convinced she could not trust or lean on anyone—that she pushed away the very stability she desired. The blessing she wanted began to feel out of reach. That frustration made her even more prone to lashing out, not because she didn't want love, but because her mindset had not yet shifted to receive it. She was pleading with God for a gift her heart had no space to hold.

Maybe you've been there too—asking God for something good, only to wonder why it feels so far away. Sometimes the distance isn't about God withholding; it's about us still carrying the old scripts that tell us we can't handle what we're asking for. Healing often opens our eyes and hearts to notice, receive, and sustain what God has already placed in our lives. It softens our grip on fear, reshapes how we see ourselves, and makes room for blessings that once felt impossible.

This is where healing becomes more than self-help. It's not about "fixing yourself" so you can earn love or worthiness. It's about allowing God to transform the way you see yourself, so you can step fully into the life and relationships you were created for.

Paul put it this way in Romans 12:2: "Be transformed by the renewing of your mind." Healing requires us to release the false scripts of "I am unworthy" or "I am too much" and embrace the truth of who God says we are: beloved, chosen, fearfully and wonderfully made.

A Communal Framework for Healing

At its heart, healing is never just an individual project. We were created for connection, and our survival as a people has always depended on it. This stands in sharp contrast to the Western ideal of rugged individualism, the idea that we should pull ourselves up by our bootstraps, prove our worth through independence, and carry our burdens alone. That narrative has left many of us feeling isolated, ashamed, and exhausted, especially when we cannot live up to such impossible standards. Our tradition, however, tells a different story: we are stronger together.

This truth is already woven into the rhythms of Black life in America. We see it in the way church mothers and elders have guided entire congregations, offering wisdom and correction that extended beyond their own households. We hear it in the saying, "It takes a village to raise a child," which has never been just a proverb for us but a lived reality—grandmothers, aunties, neighbors, and godparents stepping in to nurture and protect. We see it in the history of Black mutual aid societies that pooled resources so no one went without, in the neighborhood barbershops and beauty salons that became sanctuaries of truth-telling and laughter, and in the kitchen-table wisdom passed down late at night over collard greens and cornbread.

These practices were not luxuries. They were survival strategies forged in the crucible of oppression. When systemic racism closed doors, our communities built windows of care and connection. Over time, those survival strategies became cultural anchors—reminders that we flourish when we are deeply connected.

Serena began to discover this for herself when she joined a women's support group at her church. At first, she was guarded, convinced no one would understand her fears of abandonment. But as she listened, she realized her struggles were not hers alone. One woman spoke of pushing people away because she had never felt safe to be vulnerable. Another described the suffocating silence she had grown up with, and how it still shaped her marriage. In their honesty, Serena found pieces of herself being reflected.

For the first time in a long while, she didn't feel broken beyond repair. She felt human. She began to understand that healing wasn't something she had to muscle through in private. It was something that happened in the presence of others. In the nods of recognition, the shared prayers, the gentle accountability. She felt seen. Her pain, instead of setting her apart, connected her to others who had walked similar roads.

This is why community matters so deeply for healing. We were never meant to recover from trauma in isolation. Healing doesn't come from fixing ourselves in private and then presenting a polished version of who we are. It comes from showing up—brokenness and all—within community, and allowing others to walk with us. It is a reflection of how God designed us: to love one another, to carry one another's burdens, and to be restored not only as individuals but as a people (Galatians 6:2).

Healing begins with honesty—the courage to face what hurts instead of burying it. For many of us, collective trauma has shown up as immobilizing sadness, racing anxiety, or the heavy fog of depression. These emotions are not signs of weakness. They are signals of what we've endured. The first step toward healing is naming them: I feel lonely. I feel afraid. I feel stuck. When we silence those feelings, they don't disappear; they harden into barriers that keep us from the love and connection God intended for us.

Serena discovered this in her support group. For years she kept her fears to herself, believing it was safer to remain quiet. But one evening, she surprised herself when she blurted out through tears, "I don't trust people to stay. And it makes me so tired." The room grew still—not with judgment, but with recognition. Women nodded. A few reached for her hand. In that circle, Serena found what she had been missing: her pain didn't have to isolate her. When she finally spoke it aloud, others bore it with her.

This is why healing is sacred work. It requires witnesses. God never designed us to heal alone. Counselors and therapists can walk with us in our private battles. Support groups and church communities can remind us that we are not the only ones carrying grief. Even chosen family—the friends who become sisters and brothers— can reflect God's love back to us when we forget it for ourselves.

The book of Hebrews describes the "great cloud of witnesses" surrounding us as we run this race of faith. Our ancestors are part of that testimony—not as objects of worship, but as living reminders that endurance runs through our bloodline. Their survival whispers: You are not the first to walk this hard road, and you will not be the last.

This stands in stark contrast to what we've been taught in the dominant culture—that strength means going it alone. Many of us have been praised for being hyper-independent, but often that posture is just a trauma response. I don't need anyone. I can handle it myself. That may have protected us for a season, but it also keeps us locked in isolation.

Yet in the traditions of our people, we see another way. We've always known that strength is meant to be shared: from the elders who guided whole congregations, to the neighbors who kept an eye on each other's children, to the informal gathering places that became safe harbors of joy. This communal care is not a rival to faith—it is a reflection of it.

Seeking Therapy: Choosing a Safe Guide

Healing often happens in circles. We find strength in family, in faith communities, in support groups, in friends who hold space for our pain. Communal healing is sacred and necessary. But it is not the only path. Sometimes we also need the focused, individual support of a therapist — someone trained to walk with us through the deeper valleys.

Seeking therapy can be an essential step toward healing and growth. In therapy, you have the opportunity to address emotional challenges, trauma, and mental health concerns in a supportive and non-judgmental environment. If you've never been to therapy before — and if no one you know has ever gone — hesitation is normal. Add to that the weight of systemic racism, stigma in some church communities, or personal experiences of abuse, and stepping into a counseling office can feel overwhelming.

That's why it is so important to remember this: you have rights in therapy. Therapy should never replicate the harm you've already endured. It should be a safe and welcoming space where your story is honored and your dignity upheld. Here are some fundamentals to keep in mind:

Physical Comfort and Safety: You have the right to feel physically welcome and safe during sessions. This means the therapist provides an environment that accommodates your needs, respects your physical boundaries, and helps you feel at ease.

Confidentiality and Privacy: Confidentiality is the bedrock of trust. What you share should remain private, except for the limited situations required by law (which a good therapist will explain clearly at the start).

A Non-Judgmental Atmosphere: You have the right to be met with acceptance rather than judgment — no matter your thoughts, feelings, or past. A skilled therapist supports and validates; they don't condemn or shame.

Honest Communication without Fear: Your voice matters. You have the right to speak freely, ask questions, and share openly without fear of criticism or retaliation.

Active Listening and Presence: A therapist should be fully present, listening deeply and responding with empathy. Your story deserves their full attention.

Choosing the Right Fit

Not every therapist will be the right match for you — and that's okay. Look for someone who is both trauma-informed (understanding how trauma affects the body, mind, and spirit) and culturally responsive (honoring your faith, heritage, and lived experiences). If you meet with someone and the fit doesn't feel safe or supportive, you have permission to switch. Therapy is for your healing, not theirs.

Remember

- Therapy is one tool among many. God can work through prayer, through community, and also through the wisdom and skill of trained helpers.
- You are worthy of care that respects your dignity.
- If therapy hasn't felt safe in the past, know that a different therapist — or a different approach — can make all the difference.

Daily Practices that Sustain Change

Healing does not happen in a single breakthrough moment. It is lived out in the quiet, ordinary choices of our days. Change sticks when we build habits slowly. Small steps that, over time, reshape the way we think, move, and live. Prayer, journaling, therapy homework, exercise, rest—these may not feel dramatic, but repeated consistently, they create lasting transformation.

Think of habits as building blocks. One brick by itself may not seem like much, but stack enough of them together, and suddenly you have a wall strong enough to hold you up. Healing works the same way: one deep breath, one reframed thought, one honest conversation, one night of good sleep. These small acts, when practiced faithfully, become the scaffolding for a new life. Don't overlook the basics: sleep, nutrition, and movement are not luxuries — they are forms of spiritual work, grounding your body so your emotions have room to settle and heal. Pick one habit and make it SMART: specific, measurable, actionable, realistic, and time-bound. For example: '5 minutes of paced breathing in the car before work, Monday through Friday.' Clarity makes habits stick.

How do you know a practice is helping? Look for small but concrete signs. Progress is measured in inches, not miles:

- It takes less time to return to calm after a trigger.
- You send fewer anxious texts or calls in moments of panic.
- You state one boundary calmly each week.

A gentle reminder: if you live with dissociation or trauma triggers, start with a grounding step before moving into breathwork. Try the 5-4-3-2-1 practice — notice 5 things you see, 4 things you feel, 3 things you hear, 2 things you smell, and 1 thing you taste. Keep breath or body practices brief (10–15 minutes), and close with simple aftercare like drinking water, taking a short walk, or stretching. These rituals signal to your body that the practice is complete and you are safe.

Holistic Healing

True healing requires attention to the whole self:

- **Mind:** Shifting thought patterns, reframing limiting beliefs, and practicing self-compassion instead of harsh self-criticism.

- **Body:** Moving in ways that bring strength and joy, eating to nourish rather than punish, resting when you are weary.

- **Spirit:** Returning to God in prayer, holding fast to Scripture, finding strength in rituals of remembrance, and making room for joy through laughter, music, and fellowship.

Each of these areas feeds the others. A rested body strengthens the mind. A peaceful spirit steadies the emotions. A renewed mind helps the body and spirit align.

Practices of Shared Strength

Healing is sustained not just by personal habits, but by collective ones. Our communities have always known the power of gathering around a table, whether for Sunday dinner or potluck after church. A meal shared is more than food, it is connection, a reminder that you are not alone. Storytelling circles, whether formal or spontaneous, let us hear our lives echoed in one another's voices. Accountability partnerships—trusted friends who can call us back when we drift—remind us that healing is not meant to be a solo project.

Serena began to taste this rhythm of shared strength. On nights when she felt the urge to send anxious texts, she opened her journal instead, pouring out her fears before God. She started walking with a neighbor in the evenings, finding that movement and conversation loosened the grip of worry on her chest. And once a week, she sat around a table with her support group. They laughed, prayed, and sometimes cried together. Each practice was small on its own. But together, they became the building blocks of a sturdier, steadier life.

Healing is not about perfection in every area. It's about weaving these simple practices into your days until they become second nature. Over time, you'll look back and realize the very habits that once felt small and ordinary have become the foundation of resilience.

Serena's practices may look different from yours, but the principle is the same: healing is sustained in the small choices that accumulate over time. And this is where you come in.

Take a moment to imagine what one or two building blocks could look like in your life. It doesn't have to be dramatic. Maybe it's setting aside five minutes in the morning to breathe and pray before the day pulls at you. Maybe it's calling a friend once a week just to check in. Maybe it's preparing a meal that nourishes you instead of reaching for what numbs you.

Reflection Prompts

Take a few minutes with these questions. Write freely, don't worry about being neat or perfect.

1. **Mind** – What is one thought pattern I want to shift?

Example: "I always fail" → "I am still learning, and growth takes time."

2. **Body** – What rhythm would help my body feel stronger or more rested?

Example: "Taking a 10-minute walk after work" or "going to bed 30 minutes earlier."

3. **Spirit** – What practice helps me connect with God's presence and peace?

Example: "Praying before I scroll my phone in the morning" or "singing along to a worship song that lifts my heart."

4. **Community** – Who could I invite to walk with me in this season of healing?

Example: "A trusted friend I can text once a week" or "joining a small group at church."

Your Building Block for This Week

If you could choose just one small habit to begin this week, what would it be? Write down one small step you feel drawn to take. Don't underestimate it, remember, a single brick laid each day becomes a wall strong enough to hold you. Write it here as a commitment to yourself:

Embracing Emotions Along the Way

One of the hardest parts of healing is learning to live with our emotions instead of fighting them. Sadness, anger, grief, joy—each one is a visitor. They come, they stay for a time, and then they leave. Trouble begins when we either push them away, pretending they don't exist, or let them move in permanently, becoming tenants in our hearts.

Healing requires a different posture: to welcome emotions when they arrive, listen to what they are trying to tell us, and then release them when their work is done. This doesn't mean we act on every feeling or let them rule our decisions. It means we stop shaming ourselves for feeling them in the first place.

Serena had to learn this lesson the hard way. For years, she treated her fear and sadness like enemies. When anxiety came, she tried to silence it with distraction. When loneliness showed up, she buried it under busyness. But ignoring her emotions only gave them more power. In therapy, she began a new practice: naming what she felt out loud. Sometimes it was as simple as saying, "I feel scared right now," or "I feel unwanted." Naming the emotion didn't make it vanish, but it loosened its grip. She discovered that emotions are like waves, they rise, crest, and eventually pass.

We are not meant to carry every feeling forever. Some emotions are teachers. Some are alarms. Some are reminders that we are alive. But none are meant to define our identity.

Now it's your turn to reflect.

Reflection Prompts

1. What emotions am I carrying that no longer belong to me?

2. Which feelings have I treated as permanent when they were only meant to pass through?

3. What might it look like to name them, breathe, and then let them go?

Redefining Identity and Wholeness

Healing is not only about loosening the grip of pain—it is about reclaiming who you really are. You are not your trauma. You are not the maladaptive patterns you learned to survive. You are not your failures, or even the moments you wish you could rewrite.

Part of healing is unlearning the old scripts that told you:

- I'll never be enough.

- I am too much.

- I don't deserve love.

- If I let people close, I'll only get hurt.

These messages may have once felt like truth, but they were lies planted in the soil of trauma. Healing means recognizing them for what they are and replacing them with new truths—truths rooted in God's love, in the resilience of your ancestors, and in the care of the community that surrounds you. And at the center of it all is Christ, who took the full weight of the world's brokenness on Himself so that you could rise whole, restored, and free.

Serena began this unlearning slowly. For years she had carried the script: "I drive people away." In therapy, she began to notice that this wasn't her identity, it was a story she had inherited from instability in her family and fear from past relationships. She started writing new scripts: "I can learn to trust." "I am worthy of love." Little by little, she began to see herself not as the girl who always ruined things, but as a woman who could grow, heal, and love in new ways.

Boundary-setting became part of that new identity. Instead of saying "yes" to everything out of fear of abandonment, she practiced saying "no" with gentleness and clarity. Accountability became another tool. With her support group, she allowed others to call her back when she drifted toward old patterns. And self-compassion—the hardest tool of all—meant speaking to herself with the same tenderness she offered her friends.

Healing, at its core, is remembering love. The love of God that declares you beloved. The resilience of ancestors who endured so you could be here. The care of the community that reminds you—you don't have to do this alone.

Reflection: Redefining Identity

1. What old script or message from my past do I need to unlearn?

2. What truth do I want to claim in its place?

3. Where might I need to set or strengthen a boundary so I can live in wholeness?

4. Who can I invite into accountability as I practice living into my new identity?

Identity Declaration

- Today, I choose to release the lie:

- I embrace the truth:

Healing is not a single destination you arrive at, but a journey you walk. There will always be new layers to uncover, new habits to build, new truths to embrace. That doesn't mean you are failing, it means you are alive.

Along the way, remember these truths:

- Healing is continuous, not a finish line.
- You do not heal in isolation—you heal in connection.
- You must shift your mindset to match your new reality.

Serena's story shows us this: she did not heal in one leap. She took shaky steps, sometimes stumbled, and then tried again. What mattered was not perfection but persistence—the choice to keep walking, even when it felt slow or small.

Reflection

1. Where am I still carrying old weight in my mind even though I've grown?
2. Who are the people I can call into my healing circle?
3. What daily practice will I commit to this week?

Once a week, set aside 10 minutes for a quick review: What helped? What hurt? What will I tweak next week? This cadence turns trial-and-error into steady progress.

CHAPTER 12

Reclaiming Blackness

Not for Play, Play

Not for play, play. In our culture, when a word comes twice, it means we want you to stop and pay attention. In West African languages like Yoruba, Igbo, and Akan, repetition is how you signal emphasis or intensity. Pupa-pupa in Yoruba means "very red," ọcha-ọcha in Igbo means "pure white," and in Akan, fɛfɛ means "truly beautiful." That same rhythm lives on in our speech today. When we say "tired, tired" or "not for play, play," we are echoing ancestral grammar. What some might dismiss as "improper English" is Africa speaking through us.

As linguist Geneva Smitherman explains in Talkin and Testifyin, African American speech patterns are rooted in African oral traditions, where rhythm, repetition, and call-and-response served as both communication and cultural memory.

So when I say reclaiming Blackness is not for play, play, I mean this is sacred work. It is not a hobby or a trend; it is inheritance and responsibility.

Take Jasmine, for instance. You met her before. The woman who tried to drown her pain in shots and strangers at the bar. That night, her trembling hands clutched car keys and cocktails, searching for something, or someone to steady her soul. What she didn't realize was that her thirst wasn't for alcohol or attention, it was for rootedness. She was unmoored, reaching for anchors in all the wrong places.

If this feels familiar…

Sometimes trauma pulls us toward alcohol or other substances to numb pain. If you see yourself in Jasmine's story, know you are not alone — and support is available. Professional help can make a difference. You might explore sober-curious communities, call a trusted friend, or reach out to resources like the SAMHSA Helpline (1-800-662-4357) for confidential support.

Earlier in this journey, I wrote about how so many of us feel cut off from lineage and land, drifting without anchor. Jasmine embodies that disconnection. Jasmine is the picture of what it feels like to be unmoored.

She drifts from one argument to the next, from one drink to another, from one stranger's arms to another's bed. Like so many of us, she is grasping for something steady, but what she finds only deepens the emptiness. She is not unlike those of us who were told our history begins with slavery, who were handed broken family trees and told to piece together our worth from fragments. She walks around with a hollow ache where rootedness should be.

But reclaiming Blackness shows us we are not as rootless as we once believed. Even when Jasmine couldn't see it, the rhythms of rootedness were close at hand. Our rootedness has always been here, close enough to touch. It's in our bones, in our laughter, in the way we still gather around music and food, and in the prayers of our grandmothers that continue to echo even now.

To reclaim Blackness is to remember that we are not starting from scratch. We are tapping into a well of resilience that has always sustained us.

And that, friends, is not for play, play.

Racial Identity Development and Loving Blackness

In Chapter 6, we walked through the stages of racial identity development: starting with internalized racism, moving through the encounter stage, immersion in Black pride, and finally toward integration—where we can honor our Blackness while navigating a complex world. These stages are not neat steps on a ladder. They are cycles we revisit, spirals we move through again and again as life presents new challenges.

Internalized racism is often the hardest to name and the slowest to release. It can show up in the way we straighten our hair before an interview, in the way we lower our voice when we're "the only one" in the room, or in the shame that creeps in when we catch ourselves loving our natural selves too loudly. It's in the stories we inherited labeled "too dark," "too loud," and "too ghetto" that still whisper in our ears even when we know better. Dismantling those messages is not a one-time event. It is the daily practice of catching the lie and choosing the truth instead.

Jasmine's story reminds us how these messages dig deep. When she looked into the bathroom mirror that night at the bar, what stared back at her was not just her own reflection—it was every stereotype she had absorbed, every insult she had swallowed, every subtle dismissal that told her she was not enough. The drink was not her only poison. Internalized racism was, too.

Loving our Black bodies, then, is more than a self-esteem exercise, it is spiritual warfare. Scripture tells us, "For our struggle is not against flesh and blood, but against the rulers, against the authorities, against the powers of this dark world and against the spiritual forces of evil in the heavenly realms" (Ephesians 6:12). When we choose to embrace the skin God gave us, we are not fighting people—we are fighting the systems and spirits that profit from our shame.

In one article I read, How to Love Your Black Body in a World That Doesn't, author Chante Owens reminded me that self-love is both personal and political. It means unfollowing media that shames our beauty, surrounding ourselves with affirming images, and seeking community that celebrates rather than critiques. Loving your body as a Black woman is liberation. It is refusing to let the forces of white supremacy write the story of your flesh.

In a world that polices our hair in classrooms, our curves in workplaces, and our skin in neighborhoods, loving ourselves is an act of holy resistance. It is fastening the belt of truth when the lie says we are too much or not enough. It is lifting the shield of faith when microaggressions fly like arrows. It is putting on the helmet of salvation when shame tries to cloud our minds. Every time we stand in front of the mirror and declare, "I am fearfully and wonderfully made" (Psalm 139:14), we are wielding the sword of the Spirit—the Word of God itself—against the lies that try to diminish us.

To love our Black bodies is to stand armored—not only for ourselves, but for the daughters, nieces, and sisters watching us. It is reclaiming every curve, scar, shade, and texture as sacred, and declaring that what God has called good cannot be cursed.

Reflection Prompt:

- How have I unconsciously devalued my own Blackness?

- Where do I still hear the whispers of internalized racism in my daily life?

- What would it mean to treat loving my body not as vanity, but as an act of spiritual resistance and freedom?

Black Spirituality as Resilience

Black spirituality has never been confined to the four walls of a church building. It is deeper than doctrine and older than denominations. It is the rhythm in our clapping, the sway in our bodies, the hum that rises when words are no longer enough. It is the moan at the altar, the laying on of hands, the shout that carries us through grief.

Black spirituality shows up in ways we sometimes don't even recognize. When we clap our hands in rhythm, when someone catches the Holy Ghost and begins to rock and wail and cry out like they are birthing something—that's not just church. That's memory. That's Africa alive in us.

When the world tried to break our people, we wrapped our prayers in rhythm and hid our hope in the shout. Even when the name of Jesus was not yet proclaimed in every tongue, the Spirit of God was already moving—preserving memory, sustaining dignity, and preparing the soil of our hearts for the gospel to take root. What looked like fragments of African cosmology were, in truth, echoes of God's presence, waiting to be fulfilled in Christ. These rhythms were not replacements for Him; they were vessels God redeemed and carried forward into the Black church.

And this is how we knew Christ was close—not only high and unreachable in the sky, but near. Present in the hush of an altar call, in the sway of a funeral march, in the memory of those who have gone before us but are still watching. The Spirit breathed through clapping hands and moaning voices, testifying that Jesus had not forsaken us. What our ancestors carried in song, movement, and ritual was not a substitute for the gospel but a living witness of how Christ meets us in our bodies, our culture, and our grief.

For some, the mention of African spirituality raises fear. Words like "witchcraft" or "pagan" can surface. But reclaiming Black spirituality does not mean replacing Christ—it means recognizing how God's Spirit preserved rhythms of resilience that slavery and oppression could not erase. The moan, the shout, the laying on of hands—these are not foreign to the gospel. They are ways the Spirit carried our people's worship and healing across time, all while keeping Christ at the center. Our bodies carry memory, and in those embodied practices, we encounter the same God who promised never to leave us nor forsake us.

Jasmine hadn't thought about church in years. To her, faith felt like another place she was told she wasn't enough. But when she visited her aunt one Sunday and slipped into the pew out of politeness, something happened. The choir started an old hymn; voices layered like waves. The tambourine hit just right, and before she knew it her foot was tapping. She wasn't thinking about theology. She was feeling. The sound moved through her chest like a heartbeat she had forgotten. She realized, for the first time in a long time, that maybe God wasn't up there frowning at her. Maybe God was right here, pulsing in rhythm, closer than her own breath.

Decolonizing Christianity

When Jasmine slipped into that pew and felt the music move through her, she was surprised. For so long, faith had been tangled with shame. Church reminded her of what she didn't measure up to—the rules, the disapproving looks, the unspoken message that her body, her choices, her whole self needed fixing. But in that moment with the choir, she wasn't hearing judgment. She was hearing a rhythm older than doctrine. She was touching a faith that felt alive in her bones.

This is what it means to decolonize Christianity: peeling away the layers of white supremacy that distorted our faith and made us doubt that God could love us as we are. For generations, enslavers used the Bible as a weapon, twisting Scripture to justify bondage. But that was never the true story of Christ. When we go back to the roots, we find that African people were present in Christianity from the very beginning.

Take Philip and the Ethiopian eunuch in Acts 8. The gospel reached Africa before it ever reached Europe. Long before Christianity was co-opted by colonial powers, it was already rooted in Africa — from the Ethiopian church in Axum to North

African theologians like Augustine and Tertullian. Decolonizing Christianity is not inventing something new; it is remembering what has always been ours. Our ancestors were worshiping Christ in their own languages, on their own land, with their own dignity. To reclaim that truth is to remember Christianity is not foreign to us—it is part of our inheritance.

For Jasmine, and for so many of us, healing faith begins when we let go of a colonized version of church that equates God with rules, shame, and control. Decolonizing faith invites us to encounter Christ as liberator, not oppressor. It calls us to embrace a faith that affirms our Blackness, honors our bodies, and remembers our ancestors as part of the great cloud of witnesses.

Cultural Approaches to Healing

In the aftermath of the Rwandan genocide, Western aid workers arrived with good intentions. They set up therapy rooms and asked people to retell their trauma in private sessions. But, according to writer Andrew Solomon, for survivors, these methods felt intrusive and re-traumatizing. As one Rwandan he spoke to put it, "Their practice did not involve being outside in the sun where you begin to feel better. There was no music or drumming to get your blood flowing again. There was no sense that everyone had taken the day off so that the entire community could come together to lift you up and bring you back to joy." Eventually, they had to ask the Western therapists to leave.

Healing rose from within the culture itself. Communities gathered in open spaces, danced, sang, drummed, and moved together. Joy was reclaimed not by analyzing the past in isolation but by entering rhythms of life that honored body, spirit, and community. They danced their way back to joy, embodying the psalmist's words: "You have turned my mourning into dancing" (Psalm 30:11).

This story is not just about Rwanda—it's about us, too. Western therapy, while deeply valuable, can feel too cold for collective wounds. Healing for us is not only in retelling trauma but in singing, rocking, cooking, gathering, moving our bodies in rhythm. These practices let our nervous systems breathe and our souls remember joy.

Jasmine caught a glimpse of this one Saturday when her cousin dragged her to a cookout. At first, she hovered near the edge, clutching a soda like a shield. But when the DJ put on Frankie Beverly & Maze, the whole crowd shifted like a wave. Before she knew it, her foot was tapping, her shoulders loosened, and she laughed— moving with her cousins in the line dance. For the first time in months, her body felt light. She realized healing didn't have to come in sterile rooms or from the bottom of a glass. It could come in joy, in movement, in community.

Reflection Prompt:

- Where has Western therapy felt too cold or incomplete for me?
- Where has culture—music, dance, food, family, ritual—brought warmth back to my soul?

- What practices of joy and movement can I reclaim as healing tools this week?

Survival Tools Handed Down by Ancestors

What Jasmine felt at that cookout wasn't accidental. It was survival echoing through her body. When our ancestors were stripped of freedom, family, and dignity, they found ways to hold on to humanity. They sang in the fields, told stories by firelight, rocked babies on tired hips, prayed in whispers, laughed loudly when laughter was all they had left. These were not small things. They were survival tools—ancestral technologies of resilience.

Science now confirms what our ancestors already knew. Singing together releases oxytocin, a bonding hormone that lowers stress and builds trust. Dancing regulates our nervous systems, shaking loose what trauma tries to freeze. Storytelling strengthens memory and identity. Breathwork—something as simple as a deep sigh—calms the body and signals safety. These practices are not just performances. They are the road to wellness.

But white supremacy has often tried to convince us otherwise. Too often, singing and dancing have been dismissed as stereotypes, mocked as "ghetto," or flattened into entertainment for others. What was once a sacred survival tool has been misnamed coonery. Yet our ancestors whisper a different story: This is medicine. This is how we made it through.

At the cookout, Jasmine didn't know any of that science. She only knew that, for the first time in months, she felt alive. The laughter, the rhythm, the call-and-response of her cousins singing along—it did something to her spirit. She went home that night without needing a drink. It was a small thing, but it was also everything. She was starting to taste what her ancestors had always known: resilience lives in the body, and joy is holy.

Reflection Prompt:

- Which ancestral survival tools show up in my own life—singing, dancing, storytelling, prayer, humor, cooking, gathering?

- How can I recognize these not as "small things," but as sacred practices of resilience?

- Where might I lean into one of these practices this week as an intentional act of healing?

Shared Cultural Memory and Belonging

One of the most powerful truths about Black culture is that it creates belonging out of loss. Enslavers tore tribes apart, scattering people who spoke the same language, who came from the same place, dispersing them among people of different languages, from difference places. But on American soil, there was a kind of pan-African cultural exchange that fused into something new. As culinary historian Michael Twitty reminds us, even the foods we prepare carry a lineage of survival and cultural fusion — recipes that trace both pain and resilience from Africa to the Americas. What emerged was a shared culture that often feels like we all grew up in the same household. African American culture was born out of rupture yet became a unifying inheritance.

That's why a game like Culture Tags feels so familiar. Whether the card says, "Won't He do it," "Fix it, Jesus," or "Who all gon' be there?"—we nod, laugh, and recognize ourselves. Our culture built a common language that connects us across states, generations, and zip codes. The inside jokes, the church sayings, the call-and-response—these are not just coincidences. They are proof that we survived by creating one family out of many broken ones.

For Jasmine, that realization started to sink in at the cookout. When her cousin shouted across the yard, "Who made the potato salad?" and the whole crowd erupted, she laughed so hard her stomach hurt. It wasn't just about food. It was about being inside a shared story where she didn't have to explain the joke, where she wasn't the odd one out. For once, she wasn't on the outside looking in. She was home.

This is what cultural belonging does: it reminds us that even when our bloodlines were broken, we were not left rootless. We inherited a collective memory, a household without walls. And every time we gather, sing, laugh, and play, we prove again that we belong to each other.

Reflection Prompt:
- When have I felt the deep "inside joke" of belonging in Black culture?
- What are the sayings, songs, or rituals that remind me "we all grew up in the same house"?

- How can I lean into those shared memories as a source of strength when I feel isolated?

Social Capital and Community Resilience

Shared memory is powerful, but it doesn't stop at inside jokes and familiar phrases. Over the years, we built systems of resilience that held us when the world would not. Churches, fraternal organizations, women's clubs, mutual aid societies, and HBCUs—these were not just institutions. They were lifelines. They pooled resources when banks shut us out, provided leadership when governments ignored us, and offered dignity when the wider culture denied it.

Sociologist Robert Putnam distinguishes between bonding social capital (the trust and strength we build within our own groups) and bridging social capital (the connections we build across groups). For Black people, social capital has always been essential. Whether through the church usher board, the NAACP chapter, the neighborhood block club, or the Divine Nine, these spaces allowed us to lift one another, to say: If the system won't protect us, we will protect us.

This legacy continues today. Look at GirlTrek, it is a powerful example of bonding social capital in action. Black women across the nation commit to walking together as an act of radical self-care. Their mission is simple: take a walk, reclaim your body, reclaim your streets, reclaim your joy. But behind that simple act is a movement of health, sisterhood, and resistance, echoing the same survival strategies our grandmothers knew.

Jasmine didn't have the language for any of this. But when her aunt invited her to join the women's ministry meeting at church, she felt something stir. It wasn't the sermons or the announcements that held her—it was the way women gathered around a new mother, signing up to bring meals, offering babysitting, slipping folded bills into her hand. It was the way the group paused to pray for a member battling cancer and then organized a carpool for her treatments. Jasmine realized this display of communal care on a higher level than just mere charity. This was community as medicine.

For so many of us, healing happens here—not in isolation, but in the web of connection. Social capital is resilience in action. It is Ubuntu made flesh: I am because we are.

Reflection Prompt:

- What networks or communities have carried me in times of struggle?
- Where am I being called to invest my time, care, or presence so that I too can strengthen the fabric of our resilience?
- How might I join or create a circle of belonging that supports healing, not just for me but for others?

Resilience as Epigenetic and Spiritual Memory

Healing is not only about what we learn, but also about what we remember. Trauma researchers remind us that trauma itself is nonverbal. It lodges in the body, often surfacing not through words but through sensations of being stuck, unsafe, or overwhelmed. But just as trauma is passed down, resilience is, too.

Epigenetic research suggests that the legacies of both suffering and strength are encoded in our very DNA. Scientists have found that trauma can alter the way our genes are expressed, shaping stress responses that can be passed from one generation to the next. For example, research led by psychiatrist Rachel Yehuda on Holocaust survivors and their descendants showed changes in the regulation of stress hormones, suggesting that trauma leaves a biological imprint that children can inherit. Similar studies have observed intergenerational effects among communities impacted by slavery, famine, and war. It is as if the body itself remembers. Epigenetics does not mean trauma is destiny; it means our biology can carry echoes of hardship, while also remaining open to healing and change.

Think of your DNA as a library of books. Epigenetics doesn't rewrite the words — it's more like sticky notes marking certain chapters: "Read this louder," "Skip this page," "Whisper this line." Stress and trauma can leave sticky notes behind, shaping how genes are expressed.

But here's the hope: sticky notes can be removed, rearranged, or replaced. Healing, safe relationships, and new experiences can change what's emphasized. Epigenetics means hardship can echo in the body — but it never has the final word.

Think about it. Suffering isn't the only thing that gets passed down. Strength does too. The same biological pathways that carry wounds can also carry wisdom. When you instinctively rock a child to soothe them, that motion echoes the enslaved mothers who rocked babies through hunger and fear. When you let out a long sigh after a weary day, your body is reaching for a pattern of release that generations before you used to survive crushing labor and endless worry. And when your shoulders loosen as the first notes of a familiar hymn or song rise in the room, you are not just "relaxing." You are connecting to a memory far older than you—a people who used rhythm and melody as medicine, who wrapped their grief in song so it would not swallow them whole.

These everyday actions may seem small, but they are sacred inheritances. They are evidence that resilience is not something you have to invent out of thin air. It is already written into your body. Your ancestors rehearsed these ways of coping so consistently, so faithfully, that you carry the imprint today. This is survival wisdom encoded in your very cells. Remember the Resmaa Menakem quote? "Trauma decontextualized in a person looks like personality. Trauma decontextualized in a family looks like family traits. Trauma decontextualized in a people looks like culture". I would submit that the same is true of resilience. Resilience decontextualized in a people looks like tradition, ritual, instinct. The rocking, sighing, singing, and gathering that we still do are more than habits—they are embodied memories of how to keep going.

What science calls epigenetic inheritance, I call God's mercy. If trauma can be transmitted through generations, then so can healing. God, in infinite wisdom, knew that the chains of oppression would try to choke us, that the weight of history would press heavy on our bones. So God allowed resilience to be carried forward in the very same vessels where pain might also reside. In this way, the body itself becomes a temple of memory—not only of wounds, but of deliverance.

Our ancestors left us more than scars. They left us survival stitched into our DNA, like muscle memory of hope. Every time we clap our hands in rhythm, we are echoing the psalmist's cry: "Let everything that has breath praise the Lord" (Psalm 150:6). When the hum of a hymn rises in our throats, it is the Spirit interceding with groanings too deep for words (Romans 8:26). When our hips sway to a drumbeat, it is not frivolous—it is embodied theology. It is Exodus lived out in motion, declaring we are still here, Pharaoh did not win.

So when we lift our voices, move our bodies, or gather in joy, we are not only remembering the past. We are participating in God's ongoing act of redemption. These actions are sacraments of resilience; ordinary acts infused with extraordinary grace. We are living proof that resilience is more than psychology—it is theology. It is the evidence of things not seen, the faith that our people have carried and passed down, body to body, generation to generation.

Recognizing this truth changes the work of healing. Instead of asking, What is wrong with me? We begin to ask, What wisdom is already alive in me? Instead of striving to manufacture resilience from scratch, we can honor what our bodies already know.

Reflection Prompt:

- What practices come naturally to me—rocking, singing, deep sighing, gathering with others—that may be ancestral memory at work?

- How does it shift my perspective to realize resilience is already present in my bones?

- Where do I sense God's mercy in this inheritance of strength?

Reclaiming Blackness is the process of dismantling the lies of internalized racism, of loving our Black bodies in a world that tries to devalue them, of discovering that faith was ours before it was twisted by colonizers. It is dancing our way back to joy, gathering as community when therapy rooms feel too cold, recognizing that our laughter, our songs, our prayers, and our rituals are not trivial but holy. However, doesn't have to be either/or. Healing can happen in the therapy room and in the circle; in trauma-informed care and in communal practice. Together, they give us the fullest chance to mend. That's why earlier I named both the rights we deserve in therapy and the rituals we keep in community—because our healing deserves every tool God provides.

Our ancestors gave us more than wounds; they gave us resilience. What the world mocked as "extra" or "ghetto" was survival science, encoded in our bodies by both biology and grace. The sighs, the rocking, the shouting, the humming, the laughter, these are not random gestures. They are sacred inheritances. They are God's mercy made visible in the body, proof that healing has always been within reach.

As you reflect on this chapter, remember you do not have to start from scratch. You are already equipped. The healing you long for is alive in your bones, in your breath, in your song, in your people. This is the treasure in jars of clay, the evidence that God has never left us.

Reflection Exercise

- What parts of Black culture or spirituality have I dismissed as trivial, when they might actually be sources of healing?

- How can I practice one of these survival tools this week—singing, dancing, gathering, praying—as a conscious act of resilience?

- What does it mean for me to see my body not as a problem to fix, but as a vessel of God's mercy and ancestral wisdom?

Lord,

Thank You for the gift of resilience woven into our bodies and spirits. Thank You for ancestors who carried hope through song, rhythm, and faith when the world tried to strip it away. Teach us to love the skin we are in, to embrace our heritage without fear, and to see every clap, every sway, every laugh as holy. May we remember that we are rooted, we are resilient, and we are Yours.

Amen.

Throw Everything at It,
But Don't Rush to the End

Healing as a Nonlinear Journey

We like to imagine that once we've "done the work," old wounds will stay closed and harmful patterns will never resurface. But healing rarely follows a straight line. It's more like a winding road, where stretches of progress are often interrupted by sharp turns back into familiar territory.

For some, the word backsliding carries the sting of moral failure. If that feels too heavy, think of it instead as slipping into "old ways." Old coping strategies, thought patterns, or fears have a way of resurfacing—especially when life feels overwhelming. Their return doesn't mean you are broken, and it doesn't erase the progress you've made. It simply means your nervous system is doing what it knows best: trying to find its way back to what feels like home, even if the home it remembers isn't the safest one for you anymore.

Scientists once observed rat pups that had been separated from their mothers. When given the chance, they scurried toward the scent and sound of the nest—even if the nest had been removed or no longer offered real safety. This instinct is called homing behavior. It's hardwired for survival: the pull toward what once represented comfort.

Our bodies and emotional selves do something similar. Human healing is far more complex than animal instinct, but the comparison helps illustrate how deeply our bodies can carry memory. Under stress, we're drawn back to the familiar—even if the familiar no longer serves us. Old habits, unhealthy relationships, patterns of self-silencing or over-functioning can feel like "home," not because they are safe or protective, but because they are known. The nervous system confuses recognition with safety, clinging to patterns even if those patterns are part of the very pain we are trying to heal from.

Think about it: how often have you found yourself drifting back to coping mechanisms like emotional eating, withdrawing, overworking, or people-pleasing even after you thought you'd moved past them? This is not proof of weakness or failure. It's the body's version of homing behavior at work. Like those rat pups, we run back to the nest—even when the nest is gone, or never truly nurtured us to begin with.

This is why change requires such patience. The pull of the old is strong, not because it's good, but because it's etched into memory. Familiarity feels like safety to the body, even when the Spirit within us knows better. Healing means gently retraining body and soul to recognize that new patterns, though strange at first, can also become home. With time, community, therapy, and prayer, we can rewire our homing instinct. We can teach ourselves to return not to fear or silence, but to peace, presence, and truth.

Healing calls for patience, compassion, and persistence. Patience, because growth unfolds slowly and setbacks are part of the process. Compassion, because shame only makes the load heavier. Persistence, because each time you notice yourself leaning into an old pattern and choose to realign, you are carving out a new path—showing your body and your spirit that another way is possible.

So if you've found yourself circling back, know this: you are not alone. That doesn't erase your progress; it proves you're human. And sometimes, even the act of circling back becomes part of how we learn to move forward.

Recognizing Pitfalls Along the Way

Every healing journey has traps—detours that look like strength but quietly keep us stuck. Two of the most common are spiritual bypass and toxic positivity. Both are often dressed up as strength or faith, but they can quietly undermine the deep work God is calling us to do.

Earlier, we met Carla—her body aching with migraines, stomach pain, and waves of nausea no doctor could explain. What she hadn't yet named was that her body was carrying the weight of fear. Since childhood, she had trained herself to keep quiet, to hold it all in. Like many of us, Carla's instinct was to put on the mask of strength. At church she would say, "I'm blessed," even when she was breaking inside. When pain flared, she whispered Scripture over herself as if the words alone could chase it away. To others, she looked resilient. But inside, her body was screaming for a different kind of honesty.

And this is where the pitfalls began to surface.

Spiritual Bypass

Psychologists Gabriela Picciotto and Jesse Fox describe spiritual bypass as the use of religious ideas or practices to avoid facing painful emotions, unresolved wounds, or relational struggles. It often sounds like: "Just pray harder," or "Everything happens for a reason." On the surface, those phrases seem hopeful. But for Carla, they became a way to sidestep the fear and grief pulsing through her body.

It's especially tempting in faith communities, where quick answers can protect status, preserve belonging, or keep us from facing judgment. But when we leap to bypass, we miss the deeper healing God invites us into. It silences us in the very places where God invites us to cry out. A bandage on an unclean wound doesn't bring healing—it only hides infection. The same is true for the soul. Carla's migraines and nausea weren't proof of weak faith. They were signals that truth was pressing to be acknowledged.

The difference is subtle but important:

- **Faith-filled resilience says:** I am hurting, and I trust that God is with me in the pain.
- **Spiritual bypass says:** If I really believed, I wouldn't be hurting at all.

God does not ask for denial. He asks for presence. He meets us in honesty.

Toxic Positivity

Carla also knew the sting of toxic positivity. When she admitted she was overwhelmed by the constant news of racial violence, a friend quickly replied, "Don't dwell on it—just focus on your blessings." The words were meant to comfort, but instead they left Carla unseen, as if her grief was somehow unspiritual.

Toxic positivity pressures us to smile when lament would be more faithful. It whispers "good vibes only" when what we need is to name injustice, to weep, to process. It insists on cheerfulness at the expense of truth.

But Scripture does not silence lament. The Psalms give us the full range of human emotion—joy and sorrow, praise and protest. "By the rivers of Babylon we sat and wept when we remembered Zion" (Psalm 137:1). "How long, Lord, will you look on?" (Psalm 35:17). These prayers are not failures of faith; they are faith in raw form. God's people have always cried out.

For Carla, healing began the moment she stopped pretending she was fine. In therapy, she allowed herself to sob without apology. The release didn't erase her pain overnight, but it was real. And real is always where healing begins.

Recognizing and Releasing Emotions

One of the most radical acts of healing is granting yourself permission to feel. That may sound simple, but for many of us it is anything but. We were taught to hold it together, to wear a strong face, to keep moving no matter what. Yet tears, sighs, and even groans are not weaknesses to be hidden; they are the body's way of speaking what words cannot. A sob, a lament, or the long exhale at the end of a weary day—these are embodied practices of healing that remind us we are human, and that our emotions deserve space.

Carla's body knew this long before her mind admitted it. Her nausea, jaw pain, and chest tightness were her body's language for truths she dared not speak. The constant fear she felt in childhood had not vanished with age. It had settled into her muscles and bones. Each migraine was like her body pleading, Will you finally pay attention? Will you finally let yourself feel what you've carried so long?

Paul's words in 2 Corinthians 4:8–9 offer a striking reminder: "We are hard pressed on every side, but not crushed; perplexed, but not in despair; persecuted, but not abandoned; struck down, but not destroyed." We've returned to this verse throughout the book, but notice again what Paul models here. He does not deny being pressed, perplexed, or struck down. He names the suffering honestly and without shame. His hope is not found in pretending suffering doesn't exist but in trusting that suffering will not have the final word.

This is the pattern of true resilience: naming the hardship fully while holding on to God's sustaining presence. To be pressed but not crushed means we can acknowledge pain without surrendering to hopelessness. It means we can allow space for tears and sighs, while knowing they are not the end of our story.

Charles Stanley once preached that the kind of prayer needed in crisis is not polite or carefully composed. It is full-throated and raw. The prayer that dares to cry out, "Lord, I don't know if I can hold it together another day." For many of us, that kind of honesty feels terrifying. We fear that if we open the floodgates, we'll unravel beyond repair.

Carla wrestled with this. At times, she avoided prayer altogether, worried her grief would overwhelm her faith. What if she unraveled and could not find her way back? What if her doubts drowned out her hope? What if God could not, or would not, handle her truth?

But God has never asked us to edit our prayers. The psalmists didn't. Job didn't. Even Jesus, sweating blood in Gethsemane, didn't hold back his anguish. Honest prayer is not collapse—it is communion. It is the holy act of placing our raw selves before the One who can hold us when we cannot hold ourselves.

When Carla finally allowed herself to pray through tears, with clenched fists and trembling voice, she didn't receive instant answers. What she found was presence. And sometimes, presence is enough to take the next breath.

A Practice for You

Take a moment right now. Place your hand gently on your chest. Inhale slowly through your nose, then release a long, audible sigh. Do it again—this time, imagine you're exhaling the weight of something you've been carrying silently.

If tears come, let them. If words rise up, whisper them. If all you can manage is a sigh, trust that it is prayer enough.

This is how we train our bodies and souls to recognize and release, to be honest about our pain while resting in God's sustaining presence.

Tools Already in Your Hands

One of the cruelest lies trauma tells is that you are powerless. It whispers that harm has stripped you of choice, that survival is the best you can hope for, that change is impossible. That voice whispers, "Why bother? You're stuck. Nothing will change." After years of carrying pain, that lie can feel believable.

But trauma lies.

The truth is that God has already placed tools in your hands. They may not look dramatic or earth-shaking. In fact, they may seem so ordinary you overlook them: your breath, the pause between one task and another, the friend who answers the phone, the hum of a song passed down through generations, the wisdom of a therapist, or the casserole a neighbor leaves on your doorstep. None of these erase the pain, but each one creates space for relief, for resilience, for repair to begin.

Think of Moses standing before the burning bush. When God called him to lead the people out of Egypt, Moses panicked. He pointed to his weaknesses—his lack of eloquence, his fear of failure. But God asked him a single question: "What is that in your hand?" (Exodus 4:2). It was nothing more than a shepherd's staff, an everyday tool of his trade. Yet once surrendered to God, that stick became a symbol of liberation, parting seas and striking rocks to bring water in the desert.

The same is true for us. Healing doesn't begin with mastering everything at once. It begins with recognizing what is already within reach—and choosing to use it with intention. A song can regulate your nervous system. A sigh can release the grief you've swallowed whole. A sister circle can remind you that you are not alone. Therapy can help you untangle old threads of fear.

What seems ordinary becomes extraordinary when placed in God's hands and practiced faithfully. Healing is not about waiting for something new to arrive; it's about seeing what God has already given you and daring to use it.

When to Reach for Extra Help

As you walk this healing journey, I want you to know when it's time to call in more support. Healing doesn't mean doing everything alone, and strength includes knowing when to reach outward.

Listen to your body. If you experience ongoing chest tightness, chronic pain, migraines, or other physical symptoms, please seek a medical evaluation as well as trauma care. Sometimes what feels emotional can also have physical causes. Body and soul both deserve attention.

Know when it's urgent. If you ever find yourself in crisis—facing thoughts of suicide, domestic violence, or dangerous withdrawal from substances—please seek immediate help. Safety must come first.

You are not alone. Here are resources that can meet you in the moment:

- **988 Suicide & Crisis Lifeline (U.S.)** — Call or text 988 anytime.
- **National Domestic Violence Hotline** — 1-800-799-SAFE (7233).
- **SAMHSA Helpline (for substance use/mental health)** — 1-800-662-HELP (4357).

You are worthy of safety and care. Reaching for help is not failure—it's faith in action, trusting that God's healing can work through people, communities, and professionals alongside your own resilience.

Therapy & Healing Modalities

For many in our community, therapy still carries a heavy stigma. Some of us grew up hearing that therapy was "for white people," or that seeking help meant you weren't strong enough. Those messages sank deep, reinforcing the idea that strength was about enduring silently rather than reaching for support.

The hesitation makes sense when you consider history. Much of modern psychotherapy was designed by white European men, and many of its early models did not take our cultural realities into account. No wonder some Black women feel a sense of mismatch when they first step into those spaces. Too often, the framework doesn't reflect our lived experiences.

And yet, therapy—when it is culturally competent and attuned—can be one of the most powerful tools for healing. Individual counseling offers a place to untangle the knots of grief, fear, and trauma. Group therapy carries something different: it echoes what our people have always known. We heal in community.

For Black women especially, group spaces often feel more natural than one-on-one sessions. Sister circles, support groups, and collective healing gatherings mirror the ways our ancestors sat together—sharing stories, singing, praying, laughing, and weeping as one. These spaces remind us of what Ubuntu teaches: I am because we are. To heal as individuals, we need to be part of a community where both giving and receiving are possible.

Therapy is not about replacing faith or culture—it is about creating room for both to breathe. In the right hands, therapy honors our resilience and strengthens our ability to live it out, not in isolation, but as part of a people who carry one another.

Breath Work & Embodied Healing

Another tool you already carry is as close as your next inhale. Breath work—whether through mindfulness, deep sighs, or the act of singing engages the body's natural ability to release stress and restore balance.

Singing, in particular, is both breath work and community work. Research shows that group singing can ease the weight of grief, strengthen resilience, and enhance well-being across the lifespan. In one study, participants in bereavement choirs reported greater mental health, improved self-esteem, and a renewed sense of connection. Another found that older adults who sang regularly experienced sharper cognition and increased joy. Music therapist Lisa Townsend puts it plainly: "Singing is a whole-body experience, creating opportunities for intentional, deep breaths and triggering the release of endorphins and dopamine." In other words, every song is both medicine for the mind and training for the nervous system.

For generations, Black communities have known this truth in our bones. We sang spirituals in the fields, freedom songs in the streets, and gospel in our sanctuaries.

Our songs were and are sacred technologies of survival. They metabolized sorrow, carried hope from one generation to the next, and reminded us that even in the valley, joy was still possible.

Sadly, stereotypes once mocked this resilience, twisting our joy into caricature, dismissing it as "coonery" or spectacle. But reclaiming song, dance, and movement as sacred practices reminds us of their original purpose: they are not entertainment; they are embodied prayers. Every stomp, every clap, every harmony becomes a way to regulate the body, release tension, and call the Spirit near.

Breath is always with us. Every sigh, every hum, every melody is a reminder that God's Spirit—the very breath of life—is still sustaining us. To breathe deeply is to declare: I am still here. I am still alive. I am still being held.

Redefining Self-Care
Too often, self-care gets reduced to candles and bubble baths. While rest and enjoyment have their place, true self-care is less glamorous—and far more life-giving. As Brianna Wiest reminds us:

"True self-care is not salt baths and chocolate cake, it is making the choice to build a life you don't need to regularly escape from."

That definition shifts everything. Real self-care looks like building rhythms that sustain you over time, not chasing short-term relief that leaves you right back where you started. Sometimes it is gentle—taking a walk, cooking a nourishing meal, setting aside time for rest. Other times, it is uncomfortable—saying no to a toxic relationship, making the doctor's appointment you've avoided, or uncluttering the car that mirrors your cluttered mind. Self-care is not indulgence; it is stewardship of body, mind, and spirit.

This kind of care rarely feels like luxury. It is often gritty, ordinary, and inconvenient. It might mean:

- Getting enough sleep, even when the to-do list is unfinished.
- Creating a budget or spreadsheet to get a handle on debt.
- Decluttering the inbox or unsubscribing from emails that drain your energy.
- Having the hard conversation you've been avoiding.
- Choosing vegetables over comfort food when you know your body needs the fuel.

These practices may not make for glossy Instagram posts, but they build the kind of resilience that lasts. They train us to stop running from our lives and instead participate in reshaping them.

Self-care, at its core, is parenting yourself with wisdom. It is telling the truth about what you need, making choices your future self will thank you for, and building a foundation you don't have to constantly escape. It may disappoint others who expect you to always say yes. It may require sacrifice and discipline. But over time, it creates a life that feels more livable, more aligned, more whole.

This is why real self-care is a form of resistance. For Black women especially, choosing rest, nourishment, and boundaries pushes back against a world that profits from our exhaustion. It declares: I am not disposable. My body and my spirit are worth tending to.

A Practice for You

Step 1: Reflection

Pause for a moment and ask yourself:

- What is already in my hand?
- What tools, supports, or practices do I already have access to that I may be overlooking?

Examples might include:

- A supportive friend or mentor
- A journal and pen
- Breath and the ability to pause
- A favorite song or playlist that grounds you
- Prayer or Scripture
- A healing space like therapy, group support, or a sister circle

Step 2: Identify Your Tools

Write down at least three tools you already have:

1.

2.

3.

Step 3: Choose One Intentionally

Circle or highlight one tool from your list. This week, commit to using it with intention. For example:

- If you chose breath, spend five minutes each day noticing your inhales and exhales.

- If you chose a song, let yourself listen fully and notice how your body responds.

- If you chose a friend, send them a text or schedule time to connect.

Step 4: Journal Prompt

Reflect on the following:

- How does it feel to recognize that God has already placed tools in my hands?

- What shifts when I stop waiting for something new and start using what I already have?

Building Community and Intimacy

Healing is never meant to be a solitary project. While journaling, prayer, and breath work matter deeply, resilience is rooted in the soil of community. Circles of trust—sister groups, therapy collectives, and faith communities—give us space to be seen, supported, and strengthened. They remind us that belonging itself is medicine.

Sobonfu Somé once wrote: "The goal of the community is to make sure that each member of the community is heard and is properly giving the gifts he has brought to this world. Without this giving, the community dies. And without the community, the individual is left without a place where he can contribute." Her words echo what we've already explored through Ubuntu: I am because we are. Community is not just comfort, it is calling. It is the place where healing emerges through reciprocity, where giving and receiving are equally vital.

For Black women especially, community has always been sacred ground. From kitchen tables to beauty salons, from church basements to protest lines, we have leaned on one another to process grief and cultivate joy. Healing happens in the collective heartbeat—through laughter, tears, testimony, and truth-telling.

But community is not just cultural; it is also protective. The Therapy for Black Girls podcast episode "How Racism Impacts Our Mental Health" captures this tension: how do we fight for justice while also protecting our spirits? The answer is not either/or. It is both/and. We need spaces that allow us to grieve racial trauma and replenish strength so we can keep showing up. Community becomes the bridge that makes justice work sustainable.

I remember this vividly during the height of COVID-19. The grief was relentless: pandemic anxiety, endless news of racial violence, fear for my loved ones. Within forty-eight hours, I had either spoken with or read posts from multiple Black women who said they were unraveling under the weight of it all. If I was honest, the same was true for me.

So I opened my backyard. I posted an invitation on the various social media platforms I use: "I need community. I need to process this with others going through the same thing. Despite technology, nothing replaces being face-to-face. We can do it safely, outside, weather permitting. Five women, six feet apart. DM me if you're in."

That evening, five women came. We sat apart, but together. We laughed, we cried, we told the truth about how much it hurt to keep waking up to tragedy. The air shifted in those moments. My body felt lighter, not because the trauma was gone, but because I no longer carried it alone. That circle reminded me of what Ubuntu has always taught: healing is communal. To survive in this world, we need each other.

A Practice for You

Step 1: Reflection

Who are the people you feel safe being honest with?

List their names or roles here:

1.

2.

3.

Step 2: Action

Write down one concrete step you can take this month to strengthen your connection to community.

Examples:

- Join a therapy group

- Start a sister circle

- Reach out to your faith community

- Schedule a weekly check-in with a trusted friend

My step:

Step 3: Journal Prompt

Take a few minutes to reflect and write:

- How do I experience healing differently when I am with others compared to when I am alone?

Self-Advocacy and Agency

For many of us, self-advocacy does not come naturally. From childhood, we've been trained to put others first, to keep the peace, and to be grateful for whatever scraps we're handed. We've learned—sometimes explicitly, sometimes silently—that speaking up might make us seem ungrateful, demanding, or even threatening. Better to smile, nod, and bear it than to risk being labeled "difficult."

In the Black community, these pressures are amplified by the myth of the "strong Black woman." On the surface, it sounds like praise: "You always handle everything. You're so strong." But beneath the compliment lies a trap. If strength is assumed, then our pain can be ignored. Doctors dismiss symptoms. Employers expect us to overwork. Churches lean on us to give endlessly, without offering care in return. And sometimes, without even knowing it, we pass this expectation along to one another—rewarding over-functioning and calling it strength. If you are supposed to be strong, why would you need therapy? Why would you need time off? Why would you dare to ask for more?

This script is not accidental, it has roots in history. During slavery, Black women were forced to labor under crushing conditions, often while also enduring violence and holding families together. Strength was not optional; it was survival. But what was once necessity became stereotype, and over time that stereotype was weaponized. White supremacy, patriarchy, and even our own communities have used it to justify neglect.

But resilience is not the same as silent endurance. Resilience does not mean gritting your teeth while your needs go unmet. True resilience requires the opposite—it requires courage. It requires honesty. It requires learning to voice your needs and to trust that they matter. Self-advocacy is not selfish; it is survival. It is saying: I refuse to disappear beneath the weight of other people's expectations. I am worthy of care, too.

And here's the paradox: when we advocate for ourselves, we also strengthen the whole community. Every time a Black woman dares to drop the mask of invincibility and say, "I need help," she gives others permission to do the same. Every request for rest, every boundary set, every resource claimed chips away at the systems that have profited from our silence. Advocacy is not only personal—it is collective resistance.

Carla carried the "strong Black woman" mask for years. As a student, she pushed through exhaustion until grief and stress left her unable to meet a deadline. Her first instinct was silence—pretend she was fine. But eventually, she found the courage to email her professor and request an extension. Writing those words felt like breaking a rule she hadn't realized she had been obeying her whole life.

The same pattern showed up at work. Carla poured herself into projects, adjusted to constant changes, and answered midnight emails to prove her reliability. When her performance slipped under the weight of exhaustion, her supervisor questioned her commitment. The old Carla would have apologized and doubled her effort. But this time she paused. She admitted the toll the pandemic and racial violence had taken on her mind and body, and for the first time she asked for rest—two weeks of vacation to breathe.

Her marriage revealed the same truth. For years, Carla wore a mask of capability, hiding her needs in order to avoid her husband's anger or negativity. She told herself it was safer to carry the weight alone than to risk vulnerability. Every time she bit her tongue, smoothed things over, or shouldered responsibility in silence, she thought she was protecting herself. But the mask had a cost: loneliness, exhaustion, and silent resentment that gnawed at her like a slow leak in her soul.

That habit of hiding didn't begin in adulthood—it had roots in her childhood. As a little girl, Carla learned to flinch at slammed doors, to brace herself at the sound of footsteps, to stay small and quiet so as not to trigger someone's temper. Back then, her silence was a survival strategy. She told herself: If I don't cry, if I don't complain, if I don't need anything, maybe the storm will pass me by. Those buried fears stayed lodged in her body, and no wonder she had so many "mystery" illnesses as an adult—migraines, nausea, chest tightness, jaw pain. They weren't random. They were decades of swallowed emotion, of tears unshed, of truths unspoken.

Her body had been keeping the score all along. Each time she silenced her needs in her marriage, it was like replaying the script of her childhood. Each time she said nothing to avoid conflict, she relived the same fear of being too much, too needy, too risky. The price was high: her body carried what her voice would not.

One morning, after another sleepless night, Carla stood in her kitchen, tears streaming down her face. Finally, the truth slipped out of her mouth—not as a polished statement, but as a broken whisper: "I don't want to be strong all the time. I don't want to carry everything by myself anymore."

Speaking those words, even privately, was an act of defiance against the lie that her worth depended on invincibility. For the first time, she admitted that strength had become a prison, and that what she longed for was the freedom to be vulnerable, to be held, to be human.

Paul Laurence Dunbar once wrote: "We wear the mask that grins and lies, it hides our cheeks and shades our eyes." Carla realized that her mask of strength made her look capable, unbothered, invincible. But who can add anything to someone who looks like they already have everything? By hiding her needs, she cut herself off from the possibility of receiving.

Self-advocacy is more than personal growth—it is holy resistance. It declares: My needs matter. My life is worth tending to. My voice will not be silenced. Every extension requested, every vacation taken, every trembling confession of need is a step toward freedom—not just for one woman, but for all who see her example and dare to do the same.

Facing Collective and Personal Trauma

Trauma is never only private; it is also collective, woven into the story of our people. In recent years, waves of grief have collided with one another. The murders of Breonna Taylor, Ahmaud Arbery, George Floyd, and so many others were not just national headlines—they were wounds carried in Black bodies and Black hearts everywhere. Each new tragedy did not stand alone; it pressed on scars centuries old.

Then came the pandemic, which magnified the pain. While the world trembled under fear of illness and loss, Black communities bore a double weight: disproportionate deaths from COVID-19 and the relentless reminder that our lives were still devalued. Trauma piled upon trauma. Anxiety upon anxiety.

For Carla, collective grief collided with her private struggles. Already worn thin by somatic pain and marital silence, she now woke each day to images of Black lives brutalized, replayed endlessly on her phone. She scrolled late into the night, chest tightening with each headline. Part of her wanted to look away. Another part whispered that turning away would be dishonoring the dead. The tension was exhausting: If I stop watching, I'm ignoring their suffering. If I keep watching, I can't breathe either.

This is the hidden toll of repeated exposure to racial trauma in the digital age. Our devices keep grief on a loop. Unlike generations before us, we are never given the chance to turn away, to recover, to heal before the next wound arrives. Trauma becomes ambient—always present, humming in the background of our daily lives. Our nervous systems are left raw, exposed to an unending cycle of sorrow.

And yet, in the face of relentless grief, survival tools remain. For Carla, therapy became one such tool. It was the only space where she could lay down the mask, weep freely, and name the unbearable truth: "I am not okay." Community was another lifeline. Whether in a sister circle or a virtual support group, she felt the power of collective lament—the healing that comes when you realize you are not carrying this weight alone.

Community and therapy do not erase trauma, but they create a container big enough to hold it. Alone, the weight of grief feels crushing—too heavy for one body, one nervous system, one soul. But when we enter into community or sit across from a trusted therapist, the weight is redistributed. Others help us carry what was never meant to be borne in isolation.

That is the sacred work of collective healing: to remind us that resilience is not the same as pretending to be fine. Resilience is refusing to carry the unbearable in isolation. It is leaning on the circle, on the therapist, on the Spirit who binds us together.

In the face of compounded grief, community and therapy speak back to trauma's lies:

- Trauma says, "You are powerless." Community replies, "Your voice matters here."
- Trauma says, "You are alone." Therapy says, "I see you, and I will stay with you."
- Trauma says, "You will never be whole." Healing spaces whisper, "You are already beloved, and wholeness is still possible."

Togetherness cannot undo the losses, but it changes how they are carried. Instead of drowning in silence, we are buoyed by witness. Instead of being crushed, we are steadied by shared breath. Instead of despair dictating the story, hope flickers again—passed hand to hand, voice to voice, like a candle refusing to go out.

Faith and Healing Together

Healing always asks us to hold tension. It is both now and not yet. Scripture makes this clear. In Christ, we are already made whole—declared righteous, adopted into God's family, sealed with the Spirit (Romans 5:1; Ephesians 1:13–14). And yet, day by day, we are still being renewed, still working out our salvation with reverence (2 Corinthians 4:16; Philippians 2:12–13). Theologians call this the "already but not yet" of the Kingdom. Christ's victory is complete, but we are still waiting for the fullness of that victory to be revealed.

Healing follows the same pattern. Our deepest identity is already secure—we are beloved, chosen, and free. Yet in our everyday lives, we are still stitching torn places, facing trauma, and practicing new ways of being. To live in that paradox is not contradiction; it is faith. Faith believes Isaiah's promise that "by his wounds we are healed" (Isaiah 53:5), even as we groan with Paul that "we wait eagerly for…the redemption of our bodies" (Romans 8:23). Faith holds both truths: I am healed, and I am being healed.

This tension requires humility and patience. It means trusting that while healing is God's gift, the process of living into that healing takes time. It is the seed already planted that must still grow roots and bear fruit. Paul describes this beautifully in 2 Corinthians 3:18: "And we all, who with unveiled faces contemplate the Lord's glory, are being transformed into his image with ever-increasing glory, which comes from the Lord, who is the Spirit." Notice the language—we are being transformed. Not instantly, not once and for all, but little by little, glory upon glory.

To live in this tension is to practice a resilient faith: one that can hold the certainty of God's promise and the reality of ongoing struggle at the same time. It is to wake up each morning declaring, "God has made me whole," and then choosing throughout the day to partner with God in the small, faithful steps of mending— whether that means going to therapy, praying through tears, setting boundaries, or resting when you need it.

Healing is not a quick fix but a holy process, it unfolds at different paces for each of us. And faith is what allows us to stay rooted in the promise even when the process feels long. A slower journey is not a sign of weak faith or lack of holiness; it is simply the way your story is being written.

Honest Prayer vs. Bypass Prayer

One of the most important ways we practice faith in healing is through prayer. But not all prayer is created equal. There is a difference between honest prayer and bypass prayer.

Honest prayer sounds like the psalms of lament—raw, unfiltered cries of the heart. Nearly one-third of the Psalms are laments, which tells us that God expects and welcomes our grief. Psalm 13 opens with the piercing question, "How long, O Lord? Will you forget me forever?" That is not polished or polite—it is desperate, anguished truth. Honest prayer is Hannah weeping bitterly in the temple because of her infertility (1 Samuel 1:10). It is Jeremiah crying, "Why is my pain unending and my wound grievous and incurable?" (Jeremiah 15:18). It is even Jesus in Gethsemane, sweating drops of blood, praying, "My Father, if it is possible, let this cup pass from me" (Matthew 26:39).

This kind of prayer does not pretend. It does not sanitize emotion before bringing it to God. Honest prayer allows us to bring our whole selves—anger, fear, exhaustion, and doubt—into the presence of the One who already knows. It is the vulnerable cry that says: "Here I am, Lord, and here is my truth."

Bypass prayer, on the other hand, skips over the pain. It uses polished words and spiritual clichés to avoid vulnerability. It says, "Lord, I thank you for everything," while ignoring the grief lodged in the throat. It says, "I trust You completely," but really means, "I'm afraid to admit I'm struggling." It tells us to "just be grateful" or "just trust God," without making space for lament, anger, or even doubt.

Bypass prayer may look pious on the outside—it may sound holy, especially in church settings where vulnerability feels risky—but inside it silences us. It is less about communion with God and more about performance for others, or even for ourselves. It becomes a shield we use to avoid the ache we're carrying.

But God has never asked us to silence our feelings before Him. In fact, Scripture shows the opposite: He invites us to pour it all out. "Cast all your anxieties on him, because he cares for you" (1 Peter 5:7). Not some anxieties. Not the "church-appropriate" ones. All of them. The Lord can handle our truth. He can handle our tears, our protests, our doubts, even our anger directed at Him. Honest prayer is not faithlessness—it is the deepest form of faith. It believes that God's shoulders are broad enough and His heart is big enough to carry what we cannot. And because our God is big, lament and gratitude can live side by side; naming pain doesn't cancel thankfulness, and thankfulness doesn't require denying pain.

Trusting Divine Timing

Faith also teaches us about timing. Healing is holy work, but it cannot be rushed. In our culture of instant gratification, we want transformation to happen overnight. We want our grief to resolve quickly, our anxiety to fade immediately, our relationships to mend without complication. But the spiritual life does not move at the pace of convenience—it moves at the pace of God.

There is a sacred balance between what we can do and what only God can do. We can take steps—showing up to therapy, joining a sister circle, practicing self-care, speaking up for ourselves. These are faithful acts of participation in our healing. Yet even as we act, we cannot dictate the timetable of our restoration. Healing is not a transaction; it is a process of trust.

Scripture is full of reminders that God's timing is not our timing. Ecclesiastes 3 tells us that "There is a time for everything, and a season for every activity under the heavens." Seeds do not bear fruit the day after they are planted; they must root, sprout, and grow in hidden soil before they are ready to be harvested. In the same way, healing often happens beneath the surface before we ever see evidence on the outside.

Paul encourages us in Galatians 6:9: "Let us not grow weary in doing good, for at the proper time we will reap a harvest if we do not give up." Notice the phrase "proper time." It reminds us that God's healing does not come too soon or too late— it comes at the moment it will bear the most fruit. Our role is not to control the outcome but to remain faithful, to keep tending to the soil of our lives through prayer, rest, community, and honest work.

This is why healing so often unfolds layer by layer, prayer by prayer, day by day. God peels back what we are ready to face in this season, and only then opens the next layer when we are strengthened enough to bear it. The Israelites wandered in the wilderness for forty years before entering the promised land—not because God had abandoned them, but because the journey itself was part of their formation. In the same way, our healing journeys are not detours; they are part of the transformation itself.

To trust God's timing is to surrender the illusion of control. It is to say, "Lord, I will do what I can today, and I will trust You with what I cannot." That trust allows us to stop grasping for quick fixes and instead rest in the slow, steady work of God's Spirit—the kind of work that lasts.

Integrating Faith and Therapeutic Tools

For too long, people have been told they have to choose between faith and therapy, as if one cancels out the other. In some churches, going to therapy is still treated like a lack of faith. In some counseling spaces, spirituality is dismissed as unscientific or irrelevant. But healing rarely comes in silos. God is big enough to work through both prayer and practice, both Scripture and science.

Prayer can sit alongside journaling. When you write your thoughts on paper, you are engaging in a therapeutic exercise that psychologists recommend for clarity and release. But when you invite God into those pages—pouring out prayers between the lines—your journal becomes a sacred altar.

Scripture can live in conversation with cognitive-behavioral tools. When Paul urges us in Romans 12:2 to be "transformed by the renewing of your mind," he is describing what therapists today would recognize as cognitive reframing. CBT teaches us to catch distorted thoughts and replace them with truth. Scripture gives us the ultimate truth to hold onto: "Whatever is true, whatever is noble, whatever is right, whatever is pure…think about such things" (Philippians 4:8).

Breath work can become prayer when paired with Scripture or affirmations. Inhale: "Be still and know." Exhale: "That I am God" (Psalm 46:10). Each deep breath becomes both a calming of the nervous system and a prayer of surrender. Science tells us breathing lowers stress hormones; faith tells us each breath is the Spirit of God sustaining us.

A therapy group can feel like church when truth is spoken and healing flows. James 5:16 says, "Confess your sins to each other and pray for each other so that you may be healed." In other words, healing happens in the presence of others who can witness, support, and intercede for us. Group therapy or a sister circle echoes this design—it is community care made tangible. When we integrate faith and therapy, we are not betraying one for the other—we are walking more fully into the wholeness God desires for us.

And remember, finding the right therapist is like finding the right church or community—it may take more than one try. If the first fit isn't right, that's not failure; switching is part of healthy self-advocacy.

A Practice for You

Step 1: Reflection

Where in your healing do you find yourself tempted toward bypass prayer?

Write down specific phrases, habits, or situations where you tend to cover your pain with polished words instead of honesty.

Step 2: Action

This week, set aside time to practice an honest prayer.

- Let it be raw.

- Let it be incomplete.

- Let it tell the truth of your heart without censorship.

Write a few lines of what that honest prayer might sound like:

Step 3: Journal Prompt

Reflect on this statement: "I am healed, and I am being healed."

- How does it feel in your body to say these words aloud?

- What tension or resistance rises up in you?

- How might God be inviting you to rest in that tension rather than rush to resolve it?

Carla's Story

We first met Carla at her breaking point—her body gripped by nausea, migraines, and chest pain that no doctor could explain. Her symptoms were not random. They were the echo of childhood fear, stored in muscle and bone during years of silence. For decades she wore the mask of strength, carrying everything alone, convincing herself that needing nothing was the safest way to live. But the cost was heavy: exhaustion, loneliness, and a body crying out for relief.

Carla's journey has not been quick or simple. Piece by piece, she began to name the truth she had long avoided. She learned the difference between bypass prayer and honest prayer, and for the first time, allowed herself to cry out to God without editing her words. She stepped into therapy and discovered a space where her tears were not weakness but witness. She leaned into community—sitting in sister circles where grief was mirrored and laughter returned to her like oxygen. She experimented with breath work and song, reclaiming practices her ancestors had always known were healing.

Perhaps most importantly, Carla began to find her voice. She asked for an extension at school. She requested time off from work. She whispered—first to herself, then to others—that she did not want to be strong all the time. Each act of voicing a need was both terrifying and liberating. Each time she spoke, the lie that her worth depended on invincibility lost some of its grip.

Carla's healing is still in process. Her body still carries scars, and her fears sometimes resurface. Yet she is no longer powerless. She is no longer alone. Where once her silence isolated her, now she chooses connection. Where once her body bore unspoken truths, now she listens and responds. Where once she wore a mask, now she dares to let herself be seen.

Her story does not close with a tidy ending, because healing rarely does. It unfolds slowly—layer by layer, day by day. And that is what makes Carla's journey a testimony. She shows us that resilience is not about never faltering. It is about learning to rise again, to seek support, to trust that God's presence is steady even when life feels fragile. Carla's story reminds us that healing is not a finish line. It is a way of living—ongoing, sacred, and possible for us all.

Holistic Healing and Resilient Living

Healing is not a straight path, and it is not a race. It requires patience—the willingness to "throw everything at it" while also accepting that progress unfolds slowly. Therapy helps us untangle the knots in our minds. Breath work steadies the nervous system. Prayer roots us in God's presence. Community reminds us we are not alone. Self-advocacy teaches us to name our needs. Each practice matters. Together, they form a fabric strong enough to carry us through.

Yet even with every tool at our disposal, healing cannot be rushed. Growth is more like roots pushing down into unseen soil than like flowers bursting into bloom. For a long time, it may look like nothing is happening. Old patterns may still tug at us, and grief may still feel heavy. But beneath the surface, new life is taking hold. God's Spirit is weaving restoration into places we cannot yet see.

This is the paradox of healing: it is both active and surrendered. We are called to show up with what we have—our breath, our prayers, our boundaries, our circles of trust—and to keep practicing resilience one day at a time. But the deepest transformation is God's work. God meets us in the gaps. He carries what we cannot. He strengthens what feels fragile. He completes what we begin.

The takeaway is this: your healing is not a project to finish but a life to inhabit. It is ongoing, layered, and unfolding at God's pace. Each honest prayer, each breath, each boundary, each circle of support is already evidence of resilience. Every small act becomes a seed, and God is faithful to bring the harvest in due season.

So if you find yourself growing impatient, remember: you are not behind. You are not failing. You are being formed. Healing is not perfection—it is participation. And in those small, faithful acts, God is present, whispering: You are healed. You are being healed. And I am with you in every step of the journey.

Reflection, Practice, and Prayer

Reflection Questions

Take time to sit with these and write your responses:

1. Where do I see "backsliding" in my healing journey—and how might I reframe it as part of the process rather than failure?

2. What tools has God already placed in my hands that I may be overlooking?

3. Where do I need to move from self-silencing toward self-advocacy?

4. Who can I invite into my healing circle this season?

Practice

- Choose one tangible resilience practice to commit to this week. Examples:

- Gentle movement (walking, stretching, dancing)

- Breath work or mindful sighs throughout the day

- Decluttering one space in your home, car, or digital life

- Having a self-advocacy conversation (naming a need, asking for support)

My practice this week will be:

Journal Prompt: Reflect on this statement: "I am healed, and I am being healed."

- How does it feel in your body to say these words aloud?

- What resistance or tension rises up in you?

- How might God be inviting you to rest in that tension rather than rush to resolve it?

Gracious and loving God,

We come before You with our whole selves—our weariness, our longing, our hope, and our hurt.

Thank You for reminding us that healing is both a gift and a journey,

that in Christ we are already whole even as we are still being made whole day by day.

Teach us patience with ourselves and with Your timing.

When we are tempted to rush, slow us down.

When we feel powerless, open our eyes to the tools already in our hands.

When we feel alone, surround us with circles of care.

When we grow weary, breathe new strength into our spirits.

Help us to show up fully—to pray honestly, to breathe deeply, to seek support,

to advocate for ourselves, and to trust You with the work we cannot do on our own.

May every small step toward resilience be met with Your great faithfulness.

We rest in the assurance that we are not abandoned,

we are not powerless,

and we are not alone.

In the name of Jesus, our Healer and Sustainer,

Amen.

CHAPTER 14

Blessed to Be a Blessing

Here at the end of this book, I find myself walking once more with Mama Feely. The path is familiar now—the soft rustle of leaves, the steady rhythm of her footsteps, the way she tilts her head when she's about to say something that matters. We've been on quite a journey together. My heart is heavy with all we've uncovered, yet light with the healing and hope that has emerged.

She looks at me with knowing eyes.

"Well now, chile… we done come a mighty long way t'gether, ain't we? Lemme set you down an' tell ya somethin' true: we ain't jus' blessed fo' ourselves. We blessed so we kin be a blessin' to othah folks too."

I take a deep breath and let her words sink in. She's right. These pages have carried us through the long corridors of history, across the heavy weight of trauma, and into the sacred ground of resilience and faith. We have named our wounds and remembered our worth. We have looked honestly at the forces that tried to break us and claimed the resilience that kept us alive.

We've discovered that healing is not just about surviving but about reclaiming. We've clung to faith when the world told us we had none. We've embraced resilience when despair tried to take root. We've reclaimed heritage that was stolen, silenced, or shamed. And we've stood tall in the truth that our identity and dignity are rooted in something no system can erase—we are made in the image of God.

Mama Feely leans in close, her voice tender but strong.

"'Member now, chile... all dat pain an' all dem struggles—when you look at it wid faith eyes—it turn into testifyin' 'bout God's grace an' love. An' dat testifyin'? It ain't jus' for you. Naw... it fo' de ones comin' after, too."

I nod, because I feel it deep in my spirit. Healing is never just personal, it's collective. It's ancestral. It's generational. We carry the strength of those who came before us, and we carry the responsibility to pass it forward. This week, take one step to embody that blessing. Bless one person, one place, or one practice with the love and strength you now carry. Ubuntu. I am because we are.

As you close this book, I want you to remember this: your story does not end with brokenness. It continues with blessing. When it feels hard again, return to the practices, the prayers, and the people who remind you that healing is a journey, not a finish line. You are not defined by trauma. You are defined by the God who has been faithful through it all. You are a living testimony of survival, resilience, and love. And you are never alone.

Wherever you find yourself—new to faith, healing from church hurt, skeptical but curious, or walking with a therapist—this blessing is still for you. There is room at the table, and your journey belongs in the story of our collective healing. So take what you have found here. Let it anchor you. Let it guide you. Let it bless you—and through you, let it bless others.

Lord,

We thank You for the ones who came before us, whose faith and resilience flow through our very veins. We thank You for the truth that we are made in Your image, and that no trauma, no system, no wound can take that away.

Give us courage to walk in healing, strength to stand in resilience, and wisdom to bless others as we have been blessed. May we remember that our pain is not the end of the story—Your grace is.

And may the generations after us rise up whole, rooted, and free.

Amen.

Come Home

History leaves scars. Systems wound. Families and institutions can fail us. And yet, Scripture says there is also another wound that runs through every heart: personal sin. It shows up in our anger, our envy, our selfishness, our pride. It doesn't erase the pain of what others have done, but it does remind us that we, too, stand in need of mercy.

The good news of the gospel is that Jesus carried both: the crushing weight of injustice and the heavy burden of our own sin. On the cross, He bore what we could not. In His resurrection, He opened the way home.

If you have never trusted Christ with your life, today can be the day. Scripture promises: "If you declare with your mouth, 'Jesus is Lord,' and believe in your heart that God raised Him from the dead, you will be saved" (Romans 10:9). That promise is for you.

You don't have to earn it. You don't have to fix yourself first. You only have to receive the gift He freely gives.

A Prayer You Might Pray

"Lord Jesus, I confess my need for You. I believe You died for my sins and rose again to give me new life. Today I place my trust in You. Forgive me, heal me, and make me new. Amen."

If you prayed that prayer, welcome home. Your healing journey continues, but now you walk it with Christ at your side, never leaving, never forsaking.

Appendix: Bibliography

American Psychological Association. "Understanding the Impact of Historical Trauma." APA Monitor on Psychology, February 2023. https://www.apa.org/monitor/2023/02/cover-historical-trauma.

Bacon's Rebellion. Africans in America. PBS. Accessed [date]. https://www.pbs.org/wgbh/aia/part1/1p274.html.

Baradaran, Mehrsa. The Color of Money: Black Banks and the Racial Wealth Gap. Cambridge, MA: Harvard University Press, 2017.

Brown, Kathleen M. Good Wives, Nasty Wenches, and Anxious Patriarchs: Gender, Race, and Power in Colonial Virginia. Chapel Hill: University of North Carolina Press, 1996.

Browley, Jasmine. "March 10 Is the National Day of Rest for Black Women." Black Enterprise, March 8, 2025.

Bryant-Davis, Thema, et al. "The Trauma of Racism: Implications for Counseling, Research, and Education." The Counseling Psychologist 48, no. 4 (2020): 561–93.

Cone, James H. The Spirituals and the Blues: An Interpretation. Maryknoll, NY: Orbis Books, 1991.

DeGruy, Joy. Post Traumatic Slave Syndrome: America's Legacy of Enduring Injury and Healing. Portland, OR: Joy DeGruy Publications, 2005.

Du Bois, W.E.B. The Souls of Black Folk. Chicago: A.C. McClurg & Co., 1903.

Encyclopedia Virginia. "African Americans at Jamestown." Accessed [date]. https://www.pbs.org/wgbh/aia/part1/1p274.html.

Encyclopedia Virginia. "General Court Responds to Runaway Servants and Slaves (1640)." Accessed [date]. https://encyclopediavirginia.org/primary-documents/general-court-responds-to-runaway-servants-and-slaves-1640/.

Encyclopedia Virginia. "Key, Elizabeth (fl. 1655–1660)." Accessed [date]. https://encyclopediavirginia.org/entries/key-elizabeth-fl-1655-1660/.

Encyclopedia Virginia. "Virginia Company of London." Accessed [date]. https://encyclopediavirginia.org/entries/virginia-company-of-london/.

Enright, Robert D., and Richard P. Fitzgibbons. Helping Clients Forgive: An Empirical Guide for Resolving Anger and Restoring Hope. Washington, DC: American Psychological Association, 2000.

Felitti, Vincent J., et al. "Relationship of Childhood Abuse and Household Dysfunction to Many of the Leading Causes of Death in Adults: The Adverse Childhood Experiences (ACE) Study." American Journal of Preventive Medicine 14, no. 4 (1998): 245–58.

Foner, Eric. Reconstruction: America's Unfinished Revolution, 1863–1877. New York: Harper & Row, 1988.

Fraser, Gertrude. African American Midwifery in the South: Dialogues of Birth, Race, and Memory. Cambridge, MA: Harvard University Press, 1998.

Gafney, Wilda C. Womanist Midrash: A Reintroduction to the Women of the Torah and the Throne. Louisville: Westminster John Knox Press, 2017.

Graff, Gil. "The Intergenerational Trauma of Slavery and Its Aftermath." ResearchGate, 2014. https://www.researchgate.net/publication/271597832_The_intergenerational_trauma_of_slavery_and_its_aftermath.

Hale, Thomas A. Griots and Griottes: Masters of Words and Music. Bloomington: Indiana University Press, 1998.

Harper, Lisa Sharon. Fortune: How Race Broke My Family and the World—and How to Repair It All. Grand Rapids, MI: Brazos Press, 2022.

Harris, Jessica B. High on the Hog: A Culinary Journey from Africa to America. New York: Bloomsbury, 2011.

Hening, William Waller, ed. The Statutes at Large; Being a Collection of All the Laws of Virginia. Richmond: Franklin Press, 1809–1823.

Hersey, Tricia. Rest Is Resistance: A Manifesto. New York: Little, Brown Spark, 2022.

High on the Hog: How African American Cuisine Transformed America. Directed by Roger Ross Williams and Yoruba Richen. Netflix, 2021.

Holmes, Linda Janet. Listen to Me Good: The Story of an Alabama Midwife. Columbus: Ohio State University Press, 1994.

Jennings, Willie James. The Christian Imagination: Theology and the Origins of Race. New Haven: Yale University Press, 2010.

Jenkins, Phillip. The Lost History of Christianity: The Thousand-Year Golden Age of the Church in the Middle East, Africa, and Asia. New York: HarperOne, 2008.

Maultsby, Portia K. "Africanisms in African American Music." In Africanisms in American Culture, edited by Joseph E. Holloway, 326–55. Bloomington: Indiana University Press, 2005.

Mbiti, John S. African Religions and Philosophy. London: Heinemann, 1969.

Menakem, Resmaa. My Grandmother's Hands: Racialized Trauma and the Pathway to Mending Our Hearts and Bodies. Las Vegas: Central Recovery Press, 2017.

Milgram, Stanley. Obedience to Authority: An Experimental View. New York: Harper & Row, 1974.

Mills, Kay. This Little Light of Mine: The Life of Fannie Lou Hamer. New York: Dutton, 1993.

Morgan, Edmund S. American Slavery, American Freedom: The Ordeal of Colonial Virginia. New York: W. W. Norton, 1975.

Mosley, Tonya, and James Doubek. "'Dude, I'm Done': When Politics Tears Families and Friendships Apart." NPR, October 27, 2020. https://www.npr.org/2020/10/27/928209548/dude-i-m-done-when-politics-tears-families-and-friendships-apart.

Oden, Thomas C. How Africa Shaped the Christian Mind: Rediscovering the African Seedbed of Western Christianity. Downers Grove, IL: IVP Academic, 2007.

Owens, Chante. "How to Love Your Black Body in a World That Doesn't." Healthline, July 28, 2020. https://www.healthline.com/health/how-to-love-your-black-body-in-a-world-that-doesnt.

Phillipson, David W. Ancient Churches of Ethiopia: Fourth–Fourteenth Centuries. New Haven: Yale University Press, 2009.

Putnam, Robert D. Bowling Alone: The Collapse and Revival of American Community. New York: Simon & Schuster, 2000.

Raboteau, Albert J. Slave Religion: The "Invisible Institution" in the Antebellum South. Updated ed. Oxford: Oxford University Press, 2004.

Rothstein, Richard. The Color of Law: A Forgotten History of How Our Government Segregated America. New York: Liveright, 2017.

Slave Narratives: A Folk History of Slavery in the United States from Interviews with Former Slaves. Federal Writers' Project, 1936–1938. Library of Congress. https://www.gutenberg.org/files/22976/22976-h/22976-h.htm.

Solomon, Akiba. "The Politics of Black Hair." In Colonize This! Young Women of Color on Today's Feminism, edited by Daisy Hernández and Bushra Rehman, 174–86. New York: Seal Press, 2002.

Stauffer, Rainesford. "When Family Politics Change, Every Conversation Feels Like Battle." Glamour, January 7, 2021. https://www.glamour.com/story/when-family-politics-change-how-to-cope.

Thomas, Frank A. Sermons and Lectures on Prophetic Preaching. Accessed May 10, 2025. https://www.frankathomas.com.

Tisby, Jemar. The Color of Compromise: The Truth about the American Church's Complicity in Racism. Grand Rapids, MI: Zondervan, 2019.

Truth's Table. Podcasts by Ekemini Uwan, Michelle Higgins, and Christina Edmondson. Accessed May 10, 2025. https://www.truthstable.com.

Twitty, Michael W. The Cooking Gene: A Journey Through African American Culinary History in the Old South. New York: Amistad, 2017.

U.S. Census Bureau. "Quarterly Residential Vacancies and Homeownership, Fourth Quarter 2022." Accessed May 2025. https://www.census.gov/housing/hvs/files/currenthvspress.pdf.

van der Kolk, Bessel. The Body Keeps the Score: Brain, Mind, and Body in the Healing of Trauma. New York: Viking, 2014.

Walker, Rheeda. The Unapologetic Guide to Black Mental Health. Oakland, CA: New Harbinger Publications, 2020.

Wesley, Howard-John. "God of the Oppressed." Sermon, Alfred Street Baptist Church, Alexandria, VA. Available on YouTube. Accessed May 10, 2025.

Wilkerson, Isabel. The Warmth of Other Suns: The Epic Story of America's Great Migration. New York: Vintage Books, 2010.

Williams, Delores S. Sisters in the Wilderness: The Challenge of Womanist God-Talk. Maryknoll, NY: Orbis Books, 1993.

Worthington, Everett L. Jr. Forgiving and Reconciling: Bridges to Wholeness and Hope. Downers Grove, IL: InterVarsity Press, 2003.

Yehuda, Rachel, et al. "Holocaust Exposure Induced Intergenerational Effects on FKBP5 Methylation." Biological Psychiatry 80, no. 5 (2016): 372–80. https://doi.org/10.1016/j.biopsych.2015.08.005.

Yehuda, Rachel, et al. "Influences of Maternal and Paternal PTSD on Epigenetic Regulation of the Glucocorticoid Receptor Gene in Holocaust Survivor Offspring." Frontiers in Psychology 5 (2014): 280. https://doi.org/10.3389/fpsyg.2014.00280.

Yehuda, Rachel, and Amy Lehrner. "Intergenerational Transmission of Trauma Effects: Putative Role of Epigenetic Mechanisms." World Psychiatry 17, no. 3 (2018): 243–57.

Zimbardo, Philip G. The Lucifer Effect: Understanding How Good People Turn Evil. New Y